SCHOLASTIC

Instant Homework Packets:

Vocabulary

by Jan Meyer

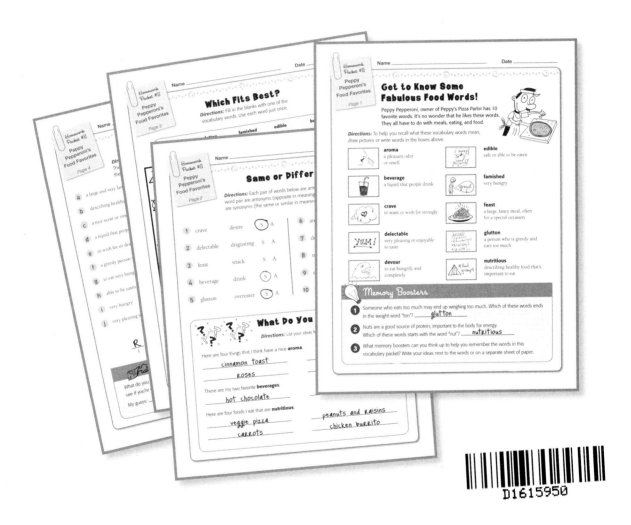

New York • Toronto • London • Auckland • Sydney
Mexico City • New Delhi • Hong Kong • Buenos Aires

Teaching *Resources*

For Jeffrey, Julia, David,
Lyndsey, Jamie, and Sierra

Editor: Sarah Longhi
Content editor: Carol Ghiglieri
Interior design: Holly Grundon
Illustrations: Mike Moran

ISBN 13: 978-0-545-13575-7
ISBN 10: 0-545-13575-3
Copyright © 2010 by Jan Meyer.

2 3 4 5 6 7 8 9 10   40   16 15 14 13 12

Contents

Introduction

A large, rich vocabulary is key to learning success. It enriches oral and written communication skills, aids reading comprehension, and boosts test scores. The goal of this book, therefore, is to help students build their word power in a fun and involving way.

In each of the 20 homework packets, students will be introduced to 10 vocabulary words that are related by a theme or specific focus. The selected words for each packet are relevant, high-utility words that they are likely to encounter over and over and in a wide variety of reading materials. To aid learning, each high-interest theme, which extends throughout the packet, provides a context for the words and their meanings.

Included in the packets are the following:

Page 1

Introduction and Vocabulary Word List

Each packet begins with a short and engaging introduction to the packet's theme or specific focus. This is followed by a listing of the packet's 10 vocabulary words and their definitions. After each of these definitions there is a small box in which students can draw a picture or write something that will help them recall the word.

For example, in the packet "Waldo the Wondrous," a student might draw a question mark in the box following the definition of the word *mystified*. In the "What's So Funny, Tucker Tickle?" packet, he or she might write the words "Ha! Ha!" in the box following the definition of the word *chortle*.

Memory Booster

This section provides a mnemonic device or a memory aid for two of the packet's vocabulary words. Students are prompted to come up with their own memory boosters as well.

In the packet "Ritzy Mitzy's Million-Dollar Words," for example, the following memory booster is given for the word *possessions*: "A dollar sign is made by writing the letter s with a vertical line through it. Some possessions can cost many dollars. Write the word *possession* using dollar signs instead of the letter s." In the packet "Lots of Nots," here is the memory booster for the word *disobedient*: "To obey means to do what one is supposed to do. Which of these words describes someone who does not obey?"

When you use these packets for homework, introduce and discuss each packet's vocabulary words and activities before students take the packet home. You might want to give a follow-up quiz on the packet's vocabulary words to assess learning.

Page 2

Synonyms and Antonyms

Most of the packets have an activity involving synonyms and antonyms of the vocabulary words. Two of the packets have an activity related to syllabication, and two have an activity related to prefixes or suffixes.

What Do You Think?

In this section learners are asked to relate several of the words to their personal experiences and knowledge.

For example, for the word *invisible*, students are asked to respond to this sentence: "Here is something I would like to do if I were invisible," and for the word *recycle*: "Here are two things that can be recycled."

Page 3

Cloze Activity

Each packet includes a cloze activity in which students must fill in the blanks with the packet's vocabulary words. To do this correctly, they must use context clues. Related to the packet's theme or focus, this section is presented in a variety of writing forms including letters, a story, and a travel journal.

Note: Be sure to remind students to read the complete sentence and surrounding information before they fill in the missing words.

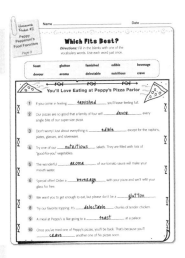

Page 4

Puzzle Activity

These fun activities are designed to reinforce the student's memory of the packet's 10 vocabulary words, their definitions, and their spelling. In many packets, these activities involve finding hidden words or answers to riddles that play off of the packet's theme. In other packets, the activity is a crossword puzzle.

Are You a Word Whiz?

In this section, students are asked to try to define a word related to one of the packet's vocabulary words. They are then instructed to consult a dictionary to see if their answer was correct.

For example, in the packet "Peppy Pepperoni's Favorite Words," one of the vocabulary words is *famished*. Students are asked what they think the word *famine* means. In the packet "The Word Artist," one of the vocabulary words is *portrait*. Students are asked what they think a *self-portrait* is.

Activities to Reinforce and Extend Learning

Here are some activities that you may want to use to help students apply and extend the learning beyond the word work presented in each of these packets.

☀ Ask students to write sentences using each of the words in the packet. Some students might want to try writing stories or letters using all or many of the words in the packet.

☀ Have students make a word card for each word in the packet. On one side, have them write the vocabulary word. On the other side, have them write a definition and, perhaps, a sentence using the word. (You will find a template for making word cards on page 89.)

☀ Ask students to use a dictionary to find other forms (noun, adjective, verb, adverb) of selected words in the packet.

Examples: **employer**, employee, employ, employment

compete, competition, competitor, competitive, competitively

migrate, migrant, migration, migratory

persistence, persist, persistent, persistently, persistency

☀ Have students use a thesaurus to find synonyms for selected words in the packet.

☀ Identify words in some of the packets that represent more than one part of speech or have more than one meaning. Such words include: prey, litter, endeavor, exhibit, assent, rustle, offense, patient, apprehend, graze.

☀ On page 90 you will find a reproducible syllabication activity. (This activity was used in the packet "Partly Cloudy and Warm.") Ask students to count the syllables in each of the packet's vocabulary words and use this page to put words with the same number of syllables in the correct geometric shape.

☀ On pages 91 and 92, you will find additional words that relate to the theme or focus of each of the packets. For some or all of your students, you may want to supplement the packets' word lists with these bonus words and incorporate them into some of the packet and reinforcement activities.

Note: A list of all of the packet words can be found on page 87.
An answer key for all of the packets can be found on pages 93–96.

Name _____   Date _____

Get to Know Some Marvelous Magic Show Words!

Wando the Wondrous puts on a spellbinding magic show! Below are ten words that may not pull a rabbit out of a hat, but are good words to know when you're talking or writing about his magic act.

Directions: To help you recall what these vocabulary words mean, draw pictures or write words in each box.

 **astonishing** – (adj.) very surprising

 **renowned** – (adj.) well-known, famous

 **conceal** – (v.) to cover up or put out of sight

 **mystified** – (adj.) puzzled or unable to understand

 **convinced** – (adj.) feeling certain or able to believe

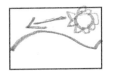 **reveal** – (v.) to bring into view

 **emerge** – (v.) to come into view

skeptical – (adj.) feeling doubt or an unwillingness to believe

endeavor – (v.) to attempt or make an effort to do something

 **vanish** – (v.) to suddenly disappear from sight

Memory Boosters

1 Which two of these words rhyme and are antonyms? _____ and _____

2 A mystery is something that is puzzling or can't seem to be explained. Which of these words starts with the same four letters as the word mystery? _____

3 What memory boosters can you think up to help you remember the words in this vocabulary packet? Write your ideas next to the words or on a separate sheet of paper.

Name _____ **Date** _____

Same or Different?

Directions: Each of the pairs of words below are antonyms or synonyms.
If the words are antonyms (opposite in meaning), circle "A." If the words are
synonyms (the same or similar in meaning), circle "S."

1. emerge   disappear   (A) S
2. reveal   show   A (S)
3. endeavor   try   A (S)
4. skeptical   sure   (A) S
5. convinced   doubtful   (A) S

6. vanish   appear   (A) S
7. astonishing   amazing   A (S)
8. renowned   unknown   (A) S
9. conceal   hide   A (S)
10. mystified   puzzled   A (S)

What Do You Think?

Directions: List your ideas for each prompt.

Here are two things that I would like to **endeavor** to do.

go the a muscam   have a bus drive

This is something that I was or am **skeptical** about.

my siehd is leaveing

Here are two things that I think are **astonishing**.

a person banding a metal stick   someone have lots
of dimands

Name _____   Date _____

Which Fits Best?

Directions: Fill in the blanks with one of the vocabulary words. Use each word just once.

| vanish(ed) | convinced | reveal(ed) | skeptical | conceal(ed) |
| endeavor | emerge(d) | astonishing | mystified | renowned |

Dear Lisa,

Last night, my family and I went to the Palace Theater to see Wando the Wondrous. He is an amazing magician who is ___renowned___ (1) all over the world. At first, my older brother, Max, was ___skeptical___ (2) because he thinks all magicians use trickery to fool the audience. But Wando was so good that soon Max was ___convinced___ (3) that the acts were truly magic.

In his first act, Wando took off his tall, black hat and then put it back on. Then, he took a parrot out of its cage and ___conceal___ (4) it inside a box. When he opened the box, the parrot had ___vanished___ (5). But that's not all! Wando then lifted up his hat and ___reveal___ (6) the parrot. It was sitting on top of his head. We were all ___mystified___ (7)!

For his last act, Wando told us that he would now ___endeavor___ (8) to escape from a small tank filled with water. Wando climbed into the tank and crouched down. Then an assistant locked the lid and put a screen in front of the tank. Everyone in the audience waited nervously. Before long, though, a dripping wet Wando ___emerge___ (9) from behind the screen. It was ___astonishing___ (10)!

Love,

Ginny

Name _____   Date _____

Discover the Hidden Words

Directions: Write the correct vocabulary word next to each definition.
Then, to find the hidden message, write each numbered letter from your answers on the matching numbered line near the bottom of the page.

a   to feel sure about something   C o n v i n c e d
                                                    10

b   famous   r e n o w n e d
                                              6   15

c   the opposite of "conceal"   r e v e a l
                                                  14

d   feeling doubts about something   s k e p t i c a l
                                                12

e   to suddenly disappear   v a n i s h
                                            9   2

f   quite amazing   a s t o n i s h i n g
                                              8   13

g   unable to understand   m y s t i f i e d
                                              1   4

h   to remove from sight   c o n c e a l
                                                        5

i   to come out from   e m e r g e
                                                3   11

j   to try to do something   e n d e a v o r
                                                    7   16

The amazing act is called

t   h   e   s   l   o   a   t   i   n   g
1   2   3   4   5   6   7   8   9   10 11

p   l   a   n   o .
12 13 14 15 16

Are You a Word Whiz?

The word *revelation* is a noun. What do you think *revelation* means? Take a guess and then look it up in a dictionary to see if you're right.

My guess: _to over throw a government_____

Name _____ Date _____

Get to Know Some Super Sports Words!

Denzel and Kimberly and their friends all love sports. Each has a favorite sport that he or she likes to play, do, or watch. They like words related to sports, too. Here are some of those words they like best.

Directions: To help you recall what these vocabulary words mean, draw pictures or write words in each box.

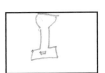 **trophy** – (n.) an award or prize given to show success

 **offense** – (n.) in sports, the team that is trying to score

 agile – (adj.) able to move quickly with ease and grace

 **opponent** – (n.) someone who is on the other side in a game or sport

 **aquatic** – (adj.) growing, living, or taking place in or on the water

 **persistence** – (n.) sticking to something and not giving up

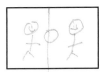 **compete** – (v.) to try to win or take part in a sport or a game against others

 **strenuous** – (adj.) requiring much effort or energy

 **novice** – (n.) someone who is new to something

 **tournament** – (n.) a series of games against competitors to find a final winner

Memory Boosters

1 Someone who is opposite you on a tennis court or whose goal is opposite yours on the soccer field is your _opponent_.

2 Which of these words starts with the first five letters of *strength* and describes a sport or activity that requires strength? _strenuous_

3 What memory boosters can you think up to help you remember the words in this vocabulary packet? Write your ideas next to the words or on a separate sheet of paper.

Strenuous because it is showing someone listing weight

Name _____   Date _____

Same or Different?

Directions: Each of the pairs of words below are antonyms or synonyms.
If the words are antonyms (opposite in meaning), circle "A." If the words are
synonyms (the same or similar in meaning), circle "S."

1. agile   clumsy   A   S

2. tournament   contest   A   (S)

3. novice   expert   A   S

4. opponent   teammate   (A)   S

5. trophy   award   A   (S)

6. aquatic   watery   A   (S)

7. strenuous   easy   (A)   S

8. compete   cooperate   (A)   S

9. persistence indifference (A)   S

10. offense   defense   (A)   S

What Do You Think?

Directions: List your ideas for each prompt.

Here are the names of two birds that are **aquatic**.

Swan   Seagull

These are two games, sports, and/or activities in which I like to **compete**.

Typing club   racing

When you are playing a sport or a game, do you like playing **offense** or defense better?

_____ Why? In soccer there are

offense and defense

_____

Instant Homework Packets: Vocabulary © 2010 by Jan Meyer. Scholastic Teaching Resources

Name _____   Date _____

Which Fits Best?

Directions: Fill in the blanks with one of the vocabulary words. Use each word just once.

trophy	persistence	opponent	agile	aquatic
strenuous	novice	tournament	compete	offense

Our Favorite Sports

Denzel: My sport is soccer, and the team I play on is amazing. When we have the ball and are playing

offense , we're practically unstoppable.
  (1)

Kimberly: Gymnastics is my best sport. I'm lucky that my body is _agile_
                                                                          (2)

because that's important when you do tumbling and flips.

Rosita: I love all _aquatic_ sports, particularly swimming and diving.
                      (3)

Noah: I really like to ski. I've only done it a few times, though, so I'm still a _novice_ .
                                                                                      (4)

Ashley: I run almost every day and I love to race. Last weekend I won a

tournament for coming in first in a long-distance race.
  (5)

Jason: Hiking is what I like to do best. It can be very _persistence_ , particularly
                                                                  (6)

when the paths are steep and rocky.

Tamika: My favorite sport is tennis. My toughest _opponent_ is my sister.
                                                          (7)

Yoshi: The sport I like best is football. My dad and I like to go to the stadium and watch the players

compete .
  (8)

Jennifer: Baseball is my favorite sport. I'm on a really good team. I think we'll win the league

trophy this year.
  (9)

Kevin: When I graduate from college, I want to play professional basketball. I know this will take lots of

strenuous and practice.
  (10)

Name _____ Date _____

Discover the Hidden Words

Directions: Write the correct vocabulary word next to each definition. Then, to find the hidden answer to the riddle, write each numbered letter from your answers on the matching numbered line at the bottom. **Riddle:** Why is a frog a good outfielder in baseball?

a living or taking place in water

a q u a t i c
‾4‾ ‾ ‾ ‾ ‾ ‾13‾

b a synonym for "beginner"

N o v i c e
‾ ‾ ‾ ‾1‾ ‾9‾ ‾

c a series of games to find a final winner

t o u r n a m e n t
‾ ‾ ‾ ‾ ‾5‾ ‾ ‾ ‾ ‾

d calling for lots of physical effort

s t r e n u o u s
‾ ‾ ‾ ‾ ‾ ‾ ‾ ‾15‾

e a person you play against in a sport or game

o p p o n e n t
‾ ‾ ‾ ‾ ‾ ‾ ‾8‾

f the act of not giving up

p r e s i s t e n c e
‾ ‾ ‾ ‾ ‾ ‾ ‾ ‾ ‾6‾

g a prize given to someone who has done well

t r o p h y
‾2‾ ‾ ‾ ‾10‾ ‾

h in sports the team that is trying to score

o f f e n s e
‾ ‾ ‾11‾ ‾ ‾ ‾

i able to move with quickness and ease

a g i l e
‾7‾ ‾ ‾12‾ ‾

j to attempt to win in a contest or game

c o m p e t e
‾3‾ ‾ ‾ ‾14‾ ‾ ‾

The answer is:

i t   c a n   c a t c h
‾1‾ ‾2‾ ‾3‾ ‾4‾ ‾5‾ ‾6‾ ‾7‾ ‾8‾ ‾9‾ ‾10‾

f l i e s .
‾11‾ ‾12‾ ‾13‾ ‾14‾ ‾15‾

Are You a Word Whiz?

The word *aquatic* starts with the Latin root *aqua*, meaning *water*. What do you think an aquanaut is? Take a guess and then look it up in a dictionary to see if you're right.

My guess: a person who does under water sports

Name _____ Date _____

Get to Know Some Earth-Awareness Words!

The Earth needs our help for a healthier future. It's up to all of us to get informed and do our part. Here are some words that you should know as you learn about this important subject.

Directions: To help you recall what these vocabulary words mean, draw pictures or write words in each box.

 **conserve** – (v.) to protect from loss or from being used up

Some one throwing a can
 **litter** – (n.) rubbish or trash that has been scattered about

 crucial – (adj.) of the greatest importance

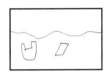 **pollute** – (v.) to foul or make dirty

 **environment** – (n.) the surrounding elements that affect living things

 **recycle** – (v.) to process old items so they can be use to make new ones

 **excessive** – (adj.) going beyond what is needed or necessary

 **toxic** – (adj.) poisonous

 fumes – (n.) gases, smoke, or vapors, especially if harmful or irritating

 **wilderness** – (n.) a wild area with no people living in it

Memory Boosters

1 The prefix *re-* can mean *again*. Which of these words starts with the prefix *re-*? recycle

2 The adjective *wild* can mean *with no people living in it*. Which of these words starts with the word *wild*? wildness

3 What memory boosters can you think up to help you remember the words in this vocabulary packet? Write your ideas next to the words or on a separate sheet of paper.

The word litter because it is showing someone No throwing the can in the recycleing bin

Name _____   Date _____

Same or Different?

Directions: Each of the pairs of words below are antonyms or synonyms. If the words are antonyms (opposite in meaning), circle "A." If the words are synonyms (the same or similar in meaning), circle "S."

1 litter	trash	A (S)	
2 excessive	required	(A) S	
3 pollute	spoil	A (S)	
4 toxic	harmless	A (S)	
5 crucial	unimportant	(A) S	

6 fumes	gases	A (S)	
7 environment	surroundings	A (S)	
8 recycle	reuse	A (S)	
9 conserve	waste	(A) S	
10 wilderness	city	(A) S	

What Do You Think?

Directions: List your ideas for each prompt.

These are four things you might see in a **wilderness** area.

Trees _____   animals _____

_____   _____

Here are two things that can be **recycled**.

_____   _____

This is what I think the environmental slogan "Don't Be a Litter Bug" means.

_____

_____

Name _____   Date _____

Which Fits Best?

Directions: Fill in the blanks with one of the vocabulary words. Use each word just once.

| excessive | crucial | recycle | litter | conserve |
| fumes | pollute | toxic | environment | wilderness |

Helping to Care for the _____
(1)

When factories dump _____ wastes into our rivers, many of the fish and
(2)

animals that live in or near these rivers are killed. These companies must be shown how to get rid of such

wastes in a safe way.

We need to reduce the amount of trash we throw away. One way is to _____
(3)

such things as newspapers, glass bottles, plastic containers, and cans so they can be treated and used again.

As the Earth's population continues to grow, we must find ways to _____
(4)

water. Fixing leaky faucets and turning off the water while we are brushing our teeth are two of the things

we can do to help.

Here are two other ways we can cut down on the amount of household waste we throw away. Buy

products that don't have _____ packaging, and carry the things we buy in our
(5)

own reusable cloth bags.

We share the Earth with plants, animals, insects, and birds. That's why it's _____ to
(6)

save and protect our _____ areas.
(7)

The _____ from the exhaust pipes of cars _____ the air.
(8)   (9)

Whenever we can, we should walk, ride a bicycle, take a bus, or share a ride in a car pool.

Thoughtless people drop _____ such as candy bar wrappers and plastic
(10)

bags on the ground. Cities need to have enough trash cans in public places, and everyone must be

encouraged to use them.

Name _____   Date _____

Reverse Crossword Puzzle

Directions: This crossword puzzle already has the words filled in. Your job is to come up with a definition, synonym, or clue* that fits each word going across or down. Then write them on the appropriate numbered lines below.

(*A clue for the word "wilderness," for example, might be "a place where you might see bears.")

```
  1            2                    3
  t            l                    r
  o   4 w  i  l  d  e  r  n  e  s  s
  x            t        5  x        c
  i            t           c        y        6 f
  7 c  o  n  s  e  r  v  e           8 c  r  u  c  i  a  l     u
               r        s           l                         m
                        s        9 e  n  v  i  r  o  n  m  e  n  t
                        i                                     s
                        v
  10 p  o  l  l  u  t  e
```

Across

4 _____

7 _____

8 _____

9 _____

10 _____

Down

1 _____

2 _____

3 _____

5 _____

6 _____

Are You a Word Whiz?

What do you think the word *toxins* means? Take a guess and then look it up in a dictionary to see if you're right.

My guess: _____

Instant Homework Packets: Vocabulary © 2010 by Jan Meyer. Scholastic Teaching Resources

Homework
Packet #4

Ritzy Mitzy's
Million-Dollar
Words
Page 1

Get to Know Some Fame-and-Fortune Words!

Ritzy Mitzy is a very rich rock star. She likes words about music, but the words she loves best relate to money and riches. Here are some of her favorites.

Directions: To help you recall what these vocabulary words mean, draw pictures or write words in each box.

acquire – (v.) to gain ownership of something

immense – (adj.) extremely large

celebrity – (n.) a person who is famous

possessions – (n.) things that belong to a person

donation – (n.) a contribution given to others, often to organizations

stingy – (adj.) unwilling to spend or give money

envious – (adj.) having feelings of desire for what someone else has

valuable – (adj.) worth a lot of money, of great value

extravagant – (adj.) spending or costing more than is required

wealthy – (adj.) having a lot of money and riches

Memory Boosters

1 A dollar sign is made by writing the letter *s* with a vertical line through it ($). Some possessions can cost many dollars. Write the word *possessions* using dollar signs instead of the letter *s*.

_____

2 *Extra* means more or beyond what is needed. Which of these words has the word *extra* in it?

_____

3 What memory boosters can you think up to help you remember the words in this vocabulary packet? Write your ideas next to the words or on a separate sheet of paper.

Name _____   Date _____

Same or Different?

Directions: Each of the pairs of words below are antonyms or synonyms. If the words are antonyms (opposite in meaning), circle "A." If the words are synonyms (the same or similar in meaning), circle "S."

1	donation	gift	A S
2	valuable	worthless	A S
3	stingy	generous	A S
4	wealthy	poor	A S
5	celebrity	star	A S

6	acquire	get	A S
7	extravagant	cheap	A S
8	envious	jealous	A S
9	possessions	belongings	A S
10	immense	tiny	A S

What Do You Think?

Directions: List your ideas for each prompt.

These are my two favorite **celebrities**.

_____   _____

Here are two things that are **immense**.

_____   _____

This is one thing that I have or that I do that might make someone **envious**.

_____

_____

_____

Name _____ Date _____

Which Fits Best?

Directions: Fill in the blanks with one of the vocabulary words. Use each word just once.

valuable	envious	possessions	extravagant	celebrity
donation(s)	acquire(d)	wealthy	stingy	immense

The Inside Scoop on Ritzy Mitzy

"I love being a _____," says Ritzy Mitzy. "Sometimes, though,"
                                   (1)

she admits, "I get tired of jetting around."

When Ritzy Mitzy was a little girl, she liked to put on costumes and sing for her family. Her favorite

_____ were a pretend microphone and a sparkly purple wig.
           (2)

Five years ago, Ritzy Mitzy arrived in California with very little money. Now, thanks to huge

sales of her hit songs, she is very _____. She lives near the beach in
                                        (3)

a beautiful house. Outside, there is a/an _____ swimming pool and a
                                                (4)

tennis court. Inside, there are many _____ paintings by famous artists.
                                           (5)

Ritzy Mitzy likes to shop and can sometimes be _____. Recently she
                                                      (6)

_____ a pair of star-shaped sunglasses with diamonds on the frames.
           (7)

Are her friends _____? "Not at all," says her best friend, Cindy. "Ritzy
                        (8)

Mitzy is never _____. She likes to treat her friends to dinner, gifts, and tickets
                      (9)

to shows."

"She's very generous," adds another friend. "Last year she made very large

_____ of her money and her time to a number of important causes."
           (10)

Name _____ Date _____

Discover the Hidden Words

Directions: Write the correct vocabulary word next to each definition. Then, to find the hidden message, write each numbered letter from your answers on the matching numbered line near the bottom of the page.

a of great worth

— — — — — — — —
       8

b a synonym for "rich"

— — — — — — —
   4

c gigantic or huge

— — — — — — — —
  6   12

d things a person owns

— — — — — — — — — — —
         9

e a contribution to something

— — — — — — —
    3

f not wanting to spend money on others

— — — — — — —
  1

g a person who is a movie star or a sports star

— — — — — — — — — —
        10

h the opposite of "give away"

— — — — — — —
    5

i costing more than is necessary

— — — — — — — — — —
         11

j wanting things that others have

— — — — — — —
 2   7

Ritzy Mitzy likes to get to the music awards . . .

— — — — — — — — — — — — .
1 2   3   4 5 6 7 8 9 10 11 12

Are You a Word Whiz?

The word *acquisition* is a noun. What do you think *acquisition* means? Take a guess and then look it up in a dictionary to see if you're right.

My guess: _____

Name _____   Date _____

Get to Know Some Popular People Words!

Top 10 Trips for Tourists!

The suffixes *-or*, *-er*, and *-ist* mean "someone who." When these suffixes are added to certain words, the words refer to people. Each of these ten words contains one of these suffixes.

Directions: To help you recall what these vocabulary words mean, draw pictures or write words in each box.

aviator – (n.) someone who aviates (flies an airplane)

exterminator – (n.) someone who exterminates (kills) pests like roaches and mice

conqueror – (n.) someone who conquers (defeats, overcomes by force)

interviewer – (n.) someone who interviews people (talks with them in order to get information)

cyclist – (n.) someone who cycles (rides a tricycle, bicycle, or motorcycle)

manicurist – (n.) someone who does manicures (cares for and polishes fingernails)

demonstrator – (n.) someone who explains by showing or doing

supervisor – (n.) someone who supervises (looks after and directs) others

employer – (n.) someone who employs (gives work and pay to) one or more people

tourist – (n.) someone who tours (travels for pleasure around a city or country away from home)

Memory Boosters

1. The word *view* can mean "what one thinks" or one's "opinion about something." Which of these words means someone who finds out a person's views about things? _____

2. When you *ex* (X) something out on your paper, you get rid of it. Which of these words means someone who gets rid of something? _____

3. What memory boosters can you think up to help you remember the words in this vocabulary packet? Write your ideas next to the words or on a separate sheet of paper.

Name _____   Date _____

The Root of It

Here are the root words for each of your vocabulary words.

manicure	supervise	exterminate	cycle	aviate
conquer	demonstrate	employ	interview	tour

Directions: Write each of these root words in the circle that displays the suffix that will correctly turn it into one of your vocabulary words. Note: For the words that end in *e*, you must drop the *e* before adding the suffix.

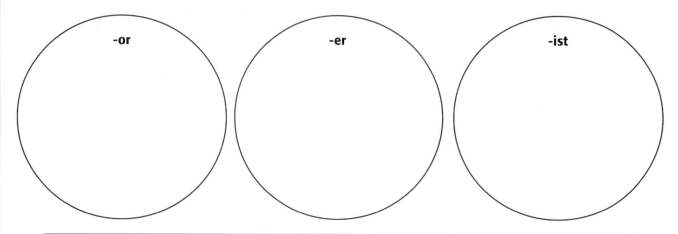

-or

-er

-ist

What Do You Think?

Directions: List your ideas for each prompt.

Here are four places where I would like to be a **tourist**.

_____   _____

_____   _____

This is something that I could **demonstrate** to others.

_____

Here are two people I would like to **interview**.

_____   _____

Name _____   Date _____

Which Fits Best?

Directions: Fill in the blanks with one of the vocabulary words. Use each word just once.

cyclist	aviator	tourist(s)	exterminator	conqueror(s)
manicurist	employer	supervisor	demonstrator	interviewer

A Who's Who of People

1 The Chu family were _____ in Washington, D.C., last month. They visited the Lincoln Memorial, the Smithsonian Museum, the Washington Monument, and many other places.

2 In the 1500s Francisco Pizarro and a group of Spanish soldiers were the _____ of the Inca Empire in Peru.

3 Bettina Bryant is a _____ in a candy factory. She makes sure that the workers put the right number of nuts in all the candy bars.

4 Daryl was a _____ in the Allegheny Mountain Bike Race last year. He came in second.

5 Tabitha Trent is a/an _____ on "Snoop," an afternoon television program. She talks with movie stars and asks them lots of questions about their lives.

6 Yousef Hassan is the _____ of five people at his sports equipment store. One of his workers makes deliveries in Mr. Hassan's company truck.

7 Kate is a _____ at Pinky's Nail Salon. Her favorite nail polish color is purple.

8 Penny Peabody is a _____ of ice-cream makers at the Kitchen Mart. She shows customers how easy it is to make ice cream at home.

9 Charles Lindbergh was a famous _____. He was the first person to fly solo, nonstop, across the Atlantic Ocean.

10 Wilbur Winston is a/an _____ for the Pest-Be-Gone Company. He works both in office buildings and in houses.

Name _____   Date _____

Discover the Hidden Words

Directions: Write the correct vocabulary word next to each definition.
Then, to find the hidden word, write each numbered letter from your
answers on the matching numbered line near the bottom of the page.

a someone who gets rid of rats
— — — — — — — — — — — —
        13   5

b someone who talks to others to gather information
— — — — — — — — — —
   10   8

c someone who hires others to work for him or her
— — — — — — — — —
                6

d someone whose job includes putting on nail polish
— — — — — — — — — —
      3   11

e someone who might show how something works
— — — — — — — — — — —
            4

f someone who is riding a bike
— — — — — — —
      1

g someone who defeated a country
— — — — — — — —
                2

h someone who is visiting a place on vacation
— — — — —
   9

i someone who oversees the work of others
— — — — — — —
                12

j someone who flies airplanes
— — — — — — —
            7

Someone who can twist his or her body into unusual positions is called a . . .

— — — — — — — — — — — — — .
1 2 3 4 5 6 7 8 9 10 11 12 13

Are You a Word Whiz?

Which of these suffixes should you use to form the word that means someone who plays
the guitar? Take a guess and then look it up in a dictionary to see if you're right.

My guess: _____

Name _____ Date _____

Homework
Packet #6

Shadowy Shapes
and Ghostly
Whispers
Page 1

Get to Know Some Great Ghost-Story Words!

In the town of Lonelyville, there was a haunted house. Those brave enough to go by the house would see shadowy shapes in the windows and hear ghostly whispers. Here are some of the words they heard.

Directions: To help you recall what these vocabulary words mean, draw pictures or write words in each box.

apprehensive – (adj.) afraid that something bad might happen

deserted – (adj.) not lived in, lonely

dilapidated – (adj.) fallen into a state of ruin, in poor condition

eerie – (adj.) strange and frightening

foolhardy – (adj.) foolishly or unwisely bold

inhabit – (v.) to live in

interior – (n.) the inside part of something

rustle – (n.) a light, soft sound of things rubbing gently together

startle – (v.) to take by surprise, to cause horror or fear

trembling – (adj.) shaking because of fear or cold

Memory Boosters

1 Someone who is frightened by something might shout, "Eek!" Which of these words starts with two *e*'s? _____

2 The word *fool* means "someone who is unwise or uses poor judgment." Which of these words has the word *fool* in it? _____

3 What memory boosters can you think up to help you remember the words in this vocabulary packet? Write your ideas next to the words or on a separate sheet of paper.

Homework
Packet #6
Shadowy Shapes
and Ghostly
Whispers
Page 2

Name _____   Date _____

Same or Different?

Directions: Each of the pairs of words below are antonyms or synonyms. If the words are antonyms (opposite in meaning), circle "A." If the words are synonyms (the same or similar in meaning), circle "S."

1	trembling	steady	A S		6	eerie	usual	A S
2	apprehensive	worried	A S		7	startle	shock	A S
3	dilapidated	sturdy	A S		8	interior	outside	A S
4	deserted	crowded	A S		9	foolhardy	careful	A S
5	inhabit	populate	A S		10	rustle	bang	A S

What Do You Think?

Directions: List your ideas for each prompt.

Here are four things in the **interior** of my home.

_____   _____

_____   _____

These are two things that I think are **eerie**.

_____   _____

Here are two things that might **startle** me.

_____

_____

Name _____ Date _____

Homework
Packet #6

Shadowy Shapes
and Ghostly
Whispers
Page 3

Which Fits Best?

Directions: Fill in the blanks with one of the vocabulary words. Use each word just once.

eerie	startle(d)	inhabit(ed)	trembling	interior
dilapidated	foolhardy	rustle	deserted	apprehensive

The Haunted House

On the edge of Lonelyville lay an area of empty, weed-filled lots and boarded-up houses. In this

_____ part of town where no one lived, there was a haunted house that
(1)

was _____ by ghosts who came out from their hiding places when it grew
(2)

dark. This spooky, old house was so _____ that it had peeling paint, missing
(3)

windows, and a big hole in the roof. Every evening, bats flew out of this hole and black cats jumped

out of the windows.

Most people were too _____ to even get near the haunted
(4)

house. But a small group of _____ teenagers sometimes dared each
(5)

other to creep up to the front door of the house on moonlit nights. When they did, they heard

_____ moans and the _____ of ghosts moving
(6)   (7)

about the rooms.

One night the teenagers tried the front door and found that it was open. They boldly decided to

explore the _____ of the house. Pushing aside cobwebs, they walked into
(8)

a large, dusty room where they were _____ by the sight of two skeletons
(9)

sitting together on an old, dirty sofa. Terrified and _____ from head to toe,
(10)

they ran out of the house as fast as they could. They never went back!

Homework
Packet #6

Shadowy Shapes
and Ghostly
Whispers
Page 4

Name _____   Date _____

Discover the Hidden Words

Directions: Write the correct vocabulary word next to each definition.
Then, to find the hidden answer, write each numbered letter from your
answers on the matching numbered line near the bottom of the page.
Riddle: What did the mother ghost say when her kids got in the car?

a   shaking with fear   __ __ __ __ __ __ __ __
                                      4   16

b   the soft sound of leaves blowing together   __ __ __ __ __ __
                                                      9 3

c   to make one's home in a place   __ __ __ __ __ __ __
                                          6   19

d   very strange   __ __ __ __ __ __
                                        17   5

e   recklessly daring   __ __ __ __ __ __ __ __ __
                                        1   7

f   worn down and in need of many repairs   __ __ __ __ __ __ __ __ __ __
                                                     18   15

g   worried about what might happen   __ __ __ __ __ __ __ __ __ __ __
                                            2   12

h   to frighten suddenly   __ __ __ __ __ __ __
                                        11   14

i   without anyone living there   __ __ __ __ __ __ __
                                           20 10

j   the inside part of a house   __ __ __ __ __ __ __
                                              13   8

The answer is:

__ __ __ __ __ __ __ __ __ __
1 2 3 4 5 6 7 8 9 10

__ __ __ __ __ __ __ __ __ __ .
11 12 13 14 15 16 17 18 19 20

Are You a Word Whiz?

What do you think *exterior* means? Take a guess and then look it up in a dictionary to see if you're right.

My guess: _____

Instant Homework Packets: Vocabulary © 2010 by Jan Meyer. Scholastic Teaching Resources

Name _____ Date _____

Get to Know Some Excellent Emotion Words!

When you describe emotions, you want to show exactly how people are feeling. In your writing, skip the boring old words like *mad*, *sad*, and *glad*—and try stronger words like *irate*, *disappointed*, and *grateful*. Here are more words that really describe feelings.

Directions: To help you recall what these vocabulary words mean, draw pictures or write words in each box.

confused – (adj.) not sure what to think, say, or do

irate – (adj.) very angry

disappointed – (adj.) feeling let down

optimistic – (adj.) looking on the bright, positive side of things

elated – (adj.) very joyful, happy, proud

sluggish – (adj.) slow-moving, without much energy

embarrassed – (adj.) uncomfortable because of something one has done

tranquil – (adj.) calm and peaceful

grateful – (adj.) thankful

uneasy – (adj.) troubled, not comfortable

Memory Boosters

1. A slug is a small creature that moves very slowly. It's slimy and looks somewhat like a snail without a shell. Which of these words is related to this creature? _____

2. To feel at ease means to feel comfortable. Which of these words means the opposite of "at ease"? _____

3. What memory boosters can you think up to help you remember the words in this vocabulary packet? Write your ideas next to the words or on a separate sheet of paper.

Name _____ Date _____

Same or Different?

Directions: Each of the pairs of words below are antonyms or synonyms. If the words are antonyms (opposite in meaning), circle "A." If the words are synonyms (the same or similar in meaning), circle "S."

1 embarrassed	uncomfortable	A S
2 tranquil	nervous	A S
3 irate	pleased	A S
4 glad	disappointed	A S
5 elated	overjoyed	A S

6 uneasy	calm	A S
7 grateful	sorry	A S
8 optimistic	hopeful	A S
9 confused	puzzled	A S
10 sluggish	lively	A S

What Do You Think?

Directions: List your ideas for each prompt.

Here are four things for which I am **grateful**.

_____   _____

_____   _____

This is a place where I feel or have felt **tranquil**.

_____

Here are two times when I felt **elated**.

_____

_____

Name _____ Date _____

Which Fits Best?

Directions: Fill in the blanks with one of the vocabulary words. Use each word just once.

disappointed	elated	uneasy	optimistic	grateful
sluggish	tranquil	embarrassed	irate	confused

I Felt So . . .

1. Mr. Franklin felt _____ when he returned to the parking lot and saw that his new car now had a big dent in its bumper.

2. Latoya felt _____ while she was sitting by the pond and listening to the birds sing.

3. Brandon felt _____ when he tried to understand the directions for fitting together all the pieces of the model airplane he was building.

4. It was a very hot day, and Max felt too _____ to go outside and play catch with his little brother.

5. Denise felt _____ when she got the hiccups in the middle of the ballet that she and her mother were seeing.

6. Juanita felt _____ when one of her friends found the bracelet she had lost in the park.

7. Jeffrey felt _____ when he was chosen to be the captain of his baseball team.

8. Sierra knew that the other teams were fast, but she felt _____ that her team would win the relay race.

9. Justin felt _____ whenever he had to walk by the old, empty house that everyone said was haunted.

10. Lindsey felt _____ because it rained on the day that they were supposed to go to the amusement park.

Name _____   Date _____

Discover the Hidden Words

Directions: Write the correct vocabulary word next to each definition.
Then, to find the hidden word, write each numbered letter from your
answers on the matching numbered line near the bottom of the page.

a how one might feel if something is difficult to understand __ __ __ __ __ __ __ __
                                                                      4

b how one might feel having spilled a drink __ __ __ __ __ __ __ __ __ __
                                                                      7

c how one might feel in a quiet, peaceful place __ __ __ __ __ __ __ __ __
                                                                  9

d how one might feel if he or she has no energy __ __ __ __ __ __ __ __ __
                                                                      1

e how one might feel if something wonderful has happened __ __ __ __ __ __ __
                                                                  10

f how one might feel if something very annoying has happened __ __ __ __ __
                                                                          5

g how one might feel if he or she hears a creepy sound __ __ __ __ __ __
                                                              2

h how one might feel if he or she lives in a nice house __ __ __ __ __ __ __ __
                                                                        8

i how one feels if he or she expects the best to happen __ __ __ __ __ __ __ __ __ __
                                                                                      3

j how one might feel if something
he or she hoped for didn't happen __ __ __ __ __ __ __ __ __
                                        6

The hidden word is:

__ __ __ __ __ __ __ __ __ __
1 2 3 4 5 6 7 8 9 10

Are You a Word Whiz?

The word *ire* is a noun. What do you think *ire* means? Take a guess and then look it up in a dictionary to
see if you're right.

My guess: _____

Instant Homework Packets: Vocabulary © 2010 by Jan Meyer. Scholastic Teaching Resources

Name _____   Date _____

Get to Know Some Nifty "Not" Words!

Disobedient Dog Makeover! At Ollie's Obedience School. Register Today!

Prefixes that can mean "not" or "the opposite of" are *im-, in-, ir-, dis-, il-, un-*. Here are ten words that have been changed into their antonyms by adding one of these prefixes.

Directions: To help you recall what these vocabulary words mean, draw pictures or write words in each box.

☐	**disobedient** – (adj.) not obedient, not doing what one is asked or told to do
☐	**displeased** – (adj.) not pleased, not happy or glad, annoyed
☐	**illegal** – (adj.) not legal, against the law
☐	**illegible** – (adj.) not legible, not easy or possible to read
☐	**improbable** – (adj.) not probable, not likely to happen

☐	**incapable** – (adj.) not capable, not having the skill or ability to do something
☐	**invisible** – (adj.) not visible, not able to be seen
☐	**irreparable** – (adj.) not reparable or repairable, not able to be repaired or fixed
☐	**unavailable** – (adj.) not available, not able to be gotten or had
☐	**uncomplicated** – (adj.) not complicated, not hard to understand or do.

Memory Boosters

1 To obey means to do what one is supposed to do. Which of these words describes someone who does not obey? _____

2 Able means having the power, skill, or means to do something. Which of these words means not being able to do something? _____

3 What memory boosters can you think up to help you remember the words in this vocabulary packet? Write your ideas next to the words or on a separate sheet of paper.

The Root of It

Here are the antonyms (or root words) for each of your vocabulary words.

capable	obedient	legal	legible	visible
probable	reparable	complicated	pleased	available

Directions: Write each of these root words in the oval with the correct prefix to form one of the vocabulary words.

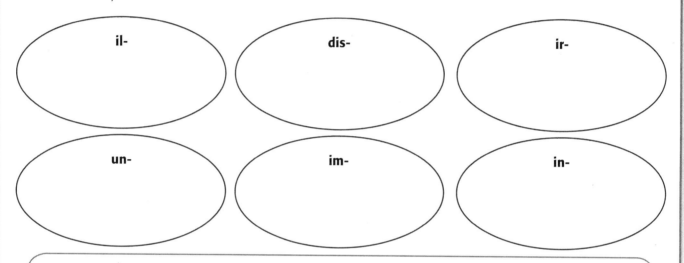

il-   dis-   ir-

un-   im-   in-

What Do You Think?

Directions: List your ideas for each prompt.

Here are two things that might be **irreparable** if they were dropped on the floor.

_____   _____

These are two things that I think seem very **improbable**.

_____

_____

Here is something I would like to do if I were **invisible**.

_____

Which Fits Best?

Directions: Fill in the blanks with one of the vocabulary words. Use each word just once.

unavailable	disobedient	displeased	irreparable	incapable
improbable	illegal	invisible	uncomplicated	illegible

Was Not, Is Not, Were Not

1. The ticket agent told Mr. Baxter that seats on today's 3:30 flight to Chicago were _____.

2. David was happy when he found that putting together the model airplane was _____.

3. Everyone was _____ when the children left their sandwich wrappers and banana peels on the picnic bench.

4. "My little brother is just like a squirmy worm," said Olivia. "He's _____ of sitting still for more than two minutes."

5. It is _____ that Jamie's new pet is a penguin.

6. When her son is _____, his mother sends him to his room.

7. It is _____ to park a car at a bus stop.

8. When Mr. Oops spilled a whole glass of lemonade on his computer, the damage was _____.

9. Ryan is right-handed. When he tries to write with his left hand, his writing is _____.

10. The wizard was _____ whenever he put on his magical purple cape.

Name _____   Date _____

Crossword Craze

Directions:
Complete this crossword puzzle by filling in the vocabulary words that fit the definitions.

Across

3 simple

6 not doing what one has been told to do

7 against the law

9 not easily read

10 unable to be fixed

Down

1 unable to be seen

2 very unlikely to happen

4 annoyed

5 not able to be had

8 unable to do something

Are You a Word Whiz?

Which of the prefixes that can mean *not* goes in front of the word *possible*? Take a guess and then look it up in a dictionary to see if you're right.

My guess: _____

Name _____   Date _____

Get to Know Some Awesome Animal Words!

Sara Safari is a zoologist. That's someone who is an expert on animals and animal behavior. Here are ten words that she thinks are important to know in learning about animals and their lives.

Directions: To help you recall what these vocabulary words mean, draw pictures or write words in each box.

camouflage – (n.) an appearance that blends in with the surroundings

hibernate – (v.) to spend the winter by sleeping or resting in an inactive state

carnivore – (n.) an animal that feeds mainly on meat

migrate – (v.) to seasonally move from one place to another

extinct – (adj.) no longer existing

nocturnal – (adj.) active at night

habitat – (n.) the place where a plant or an animal naturally lives

predator – (n.) an animal that hunts and eats other animals for its survival

herbivore – (n.) an animal that eats mainly plant material

prey – (n.) an animal hunted for food by another animal

Memory Boosters

1 A helpful way to remember which is the predator and which is the prey is to complete this little rhyme. "Go away," said the _____ .

2 The word *habit* can mean a usual way of acting or doing something. Which of these words contains the word *habit* and can mean the usual place where a particular animal is found?

_____

3 What memory boosters can you think up to help you remember the words in this vocabulary packet? Write your ideas next to the words or on a separate sheet of paper.

Name _____   Date _____

Shuffled Syllables

Directions: The second and third syllables of these words are all mixed up.
Put the correct syllables together to complete the vocabulary words.
Write the words on the lines below.

1   hab   bi   vore
2   car   ou   nate
3   pred   ber   nal
4   cam   i   tor
5   noc   a   tat
6   her   ni   flage
7   hi   tur   vore

1 _____   5 _____

2 _____   6 _____

3 _____   7 _____

4 _____

What Do You Think?

Directions: List your ideas for each prompt.

The hippopotamus feeds mainly on grasses and water plants.
Is it a **carnivore** or a **herbivore**? _____

A cat is chasing a mouse. Is the mouse the **predator** or the **prey**? _____

In May, when the rains begin to fall, the wildebeest in East Africa begin to travel north.
Are they **migrating** or **hibernating**? _____

Instant Homework Packets: Vocabulary © 2010 by Jan Meyer. Scholastic Teaching Resources

Name _____   Date _____

Which Fits Best?

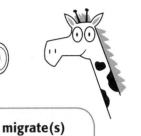

Directions: Fill in the blanks with one of the vocabulary words. Use each word just once.

camouflage	herbivore	hibernate	prey	migrate(s)
nocturnal	extinct	habitat	carnivore(s)	predator(s)

Animals Are Amazing

Each fall, the grey whale _____ from the Bering Sea in the North to the
(1)
warm waters of Mexico. This journey is 6,000 miles long!

The giraffe's _____ is the African grasslands. This
(2)
_____ eats a diet of tree leaves and twigs that are up to 20 feet above the
(3)
ground. Surprisingly, this long-necked animal has the same number of neck bones as humans.

The fur of the Arctic fox changes from brown to white as the weather starts getting cold. With

this _____, the fox blends in with the snow and ice and can hide from its
(4)
_____.
(5)

In September or October, the woodchuck seals off its underground home and begins to

_____ for the winter. It rolls into a ball, and its heart slows down to just four
(6)
beats a minute.

Like all _____, the cheetah has strong jaws and sharp teeth that can
(7)
slice, and tear flesh. It hunts for its _____ by approaching quietly and then
(8)
racing after it. This fast-running animal can reach speeds of up to 60 miles per hour in short bursts.

Most bats are _____ animals, flying about in the night hunting for food.
(9)
During the day, some bats live and sleep in caves, where there may be thousands of them crowded

together on the walls and ceiling.

Without continued and serious protection, the black rhino is in danger of becoming

_____. This very large animal has extremely poor eyesight and can
(10)
sometimes charge trees, mistaking them for threats.

Name _____   Date _____

Discover the Hidden Words

Directions: Write the correct vocabulary word next to each definition.
Then, to find the hidden message, write each numbered letter from your
answers on the matching numbered line near the bottom of the page.

a an animal that hunts other animals for food   __ __ __ __ __ __ __
                                                       6 11

b to move regularly from one area to another   __ __ __ __ __ __ __
                                                            3

c a meat-eating animal   __ __ __ __ __ __ __ __
                               9   16

d a body color, pattern, or shape that helps an animal hide   __ __ __ __ __ __ __ __ __
                                                                   13   4

e an animal that is hunted by another animal   __ __ __ __
                                                        12

f no longer living anywhere on Earth   __ __ __ __ __ __
                                            15   1

g most active during the night   __ __ __ __ __ __ __ __
                                       7

h to spend the winter in a resting state   __ __ __ __ __ __ __ __
                                                 2   10

i a place needed by a particular animal for its survival   __ __ __ __ __ __ __
                                                                       8   14

j a plant-eating animal   __ __ __ __ __ __ __
                                        5

What animal has a sticky tongue that can be about two feet long?

__ __ __   __ __ __ __ __
1 2 3   4 5 6 7 8

__ __ __ __ __ __ __ __
9 10 11 12 13 14 15 16

Are You a Word Whiz?

The word *diurnal* has the opposite meaning of *nocturnal*. What do you think *diurnal* means? Take a guess
and then look it up in a dictionary to see if you're right.

My guess: _____

   Instant Homework Packets: Vocabulary © 2010 by Jan Meyer. Scholastic Teaching Resources

Name _____ Date _____

Get to Know Some Wonderful Weather Words!

Today's Forecast:
Mostly cloudy;
light evening
drizzle.

Jack Frost is a TV weatherman. His relies on information from weather stations around the country and from weather satellites in space. Here are some of the words that Jack uses in his weather reports.

Directions: To help you recall what these vocabulary words mean, draw pictures or write words in each box.

	accumulate – (v.) to pile up, to collect little by little
	blizzard – (n.) a blinding, heavy snowstorm with strong winds
	diminish – (v.) to become smaller, to decrease, to lessen
	dreary – (adj.) dark and gloomy
	drench – (v.) to soak, to wet thoroughly

	drizzle – (v.) to rain gently with very small drops
	frigid – (adj.) very cold
	gusts – (n.) sudden, strong rushes of wind
	humidity – (n.) the amount of water vapor or moisture in the air
	sweltering –(adj.) very hot

Memory Boosters

1 The word *dim* can mean "to grow less strong." Which of these words starts with the word *dim*? _____

2 On a very hot day you may *sweat*. Which of these words starts with the first three letters of *sweat*? _____

3 What memory boosters can you think up to help you remember the words in this vocabulary packet? Write your ideas next to the words or on a separate sheet of paper.

Name _____   Date _____

Counting Syllables

Directions: Count how many syllables each of the vocabulary words has. Write the one syllable words in the circle, the two syllable words in the rectangle, the three syllable words in the triangle, and the four syllable words in the square.

| accumulate | gusts | blizzard | diminish | frigid |
| dreary | humidity | drench(ing) | drizzle | sweltering |

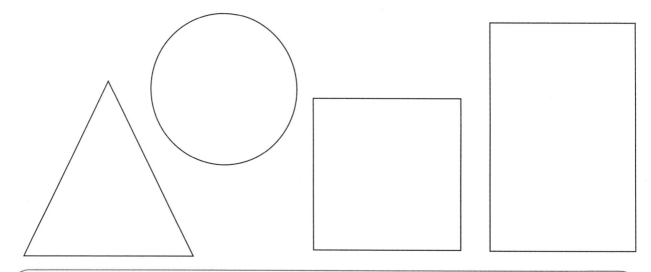

What Do You Think?

Directions: List your ideas for each prompt.

Here are four things I would wear outdoors in **frigid** weather.

_____   _____

_____   _____

These are two things I might do on a **sweltering** day.

_____   _____

What would be hard to do in a **blizzard**?

_____

Instant Homework Packets: Vocabulary © 2010 by Jan Meyer. Scholastic Teaching Resources

Name _____   Date _____

Which Fits Best?

Directions: Fill in the blanks with one of the
vocabulary words. Use each word just once.

accumulate	gusts	blizzard	diminish	frigid
dreary	humidity	drench(ing)	drizzle	sweltering

And Now Here's Jack Frost With the Weather

Winter

February 4: "Heavy snow and strong winds are headed our way. By tonight, a

_____ will close airports and make driving very dangerous. Snow may
(1)

_____ to heights of three feet in some parts of the city by tomorrow
(2)

afternoon. Temperatures will continue to be _____, with a high for tomorrow
(3)

of about five degrees above zero."

Spring

April 19: "Hold onto your hats because there will be cold _____ of wind
(4)

all day tomorrow. By Tuesday, the winds will _____, and a sunny day with
(5)

temperatures reaching into the high 60s can be expected."

Summer

August 28: "Expect another _____ day tomorrow, with temperatures in the
(6)

high 90s. With the heat and the high _____, you'll feel like you're living in a
(7)

steam bath. Take my advice, and plan to go to a long, air-conditioned movie."

Fall

October 25: "Tomorrow will be a chilly, _____ day. Better take along an
(8)

umbrella if you go out because it will _____ in the afternoon for short
(9)

periods of time. By nighttime, expect a _____ rain."
(10)

Reverse Crossword Puzzle

Directions: This crossword puzzle already has the words filled in. Your job is to come up with a definition, synonym, or clue* that fits each word going across or down. Then write these on the appropriate numbered lines below.

(*A clue for the word "drizzle," for example, might be "you may need an umbrella when it does this.")

```
¹d  r  e  ²a  r  y
           c
           c                    ³g                        ⁴d
           u                    u                         r
         ⁵d  i  m  i  n  i  s  h                          e
           r     u              t              ⁶f         n
           i     l            ⁷s  w  e  l  t  e  r  i  n  g
           z     t                             i         c
         ⁸b  l  i  z  z  a  r  d                g         h
           z     e                             i
           l                              ⁹h  u  m  i  d  i  t  y
           e
```

Across

1 _____

5 _____

7 _____

8 _____

9 _____

Down

2 _____

3 _____

4 _____

5 _____

6 _____

Are You a Word Whiz?

A weatherman predicts what the weather will be. What do you think the word *predict* means? Take a guess and then look it up in a dictionary to see if you're right.

My guess: _____

Instant Homework Packets: Vocabulary © 2010 by Jan Meyer. Scholastic Teaching Resources

Name _____ Date _____

Get to Know Some Fabulous Food Words!

Peppy Pepperoni, owner of Peppy's Pizza Parlor, has 10 favorite words. It's no wonder that he likes these words. They all have to do with meals, eating, and food.

Directions: To help you recall what these vocabulary words mean, draw pictures or write words in each box.

aroma – (n.) a pleasant odor or smell	**edible** – (adj.) safe or able to be eaten
beverage – (n.) a liquid that people drink	**famished** – (adj.) very hungry
crave – (v.) to want or wish for strongly	**feast** – (n.) a large, fancy meal, often for a special occasion
delectable – (adj.) very pleasing or enjoyable to taste	**glutton** – (n.) a person who is greedy and eats too much
devour – (v.) to eat hungrily and completely	**nutritious** – (adj.) describing healthy food that's important to eat

Memory Boosters

1 Someone who eats too much may end up weighing too much. Which of these words ends in the weight word "ton"? _____

2 Nuts are a good source of protein, important to the body for energy. Which of these words starts with the word "nut"? _____

3 What memory boosters can you think up to help you remember the words in this vocabulary packet? Write your ideas next to the words or on a separate sheet of paper.

Same or Different?

Directions: Each of the pairs of words below are antonyms or synonyms. If the words are antonyms (opposite in meaning), circle "A." If the words are synonyms (the same or similar in meaning), circle "S."

1	crave	desire	A	S
2	delectable	disgusting	A	S
3	feast	snack	A	S
4	beverage	drink	A	S
5	glutton	overeater	A	S

6	aroma	scent	A	S
7	devour	taste	A	S
8	nutritious	healthy	A	S
9	edible	poisonous	A	S
10	famished	full	A	S

What Do You Think?

Directions: List your ideas for each prompt.

Here are four things that I think have a nice **aroma**.

_____   _____

_____   _____

These are my two favorite **beverages**.

_____   _____

Here are four foods I eat that are **nutritious**.

_____   _____

_____   _____

Instant Homework Packets: Vocabulary © 2010 by Jan Meyer. Scholastic Teaching Resources

Name _____   Date _____

Which Fits Best?

Directions: Fill in the blanks with one of the vocabulary words. Use each word just once.

feast	glutton	famished	edible	beverage
devour	aroma	delectable	nutritious	crave

You'll Love Eating at Peppy's Pizza Parlor

1 If you come in feeling _____, you'll leave feeling full.

2 Our pizzas are so good that a family of four will _____ every single bite of our super-size pizza.

3 Don't worry! Just about everything is _____ except for the napkins, plates, glasses, and silverware.

4 Try one of our _____ salads. They are filled with lots of "good-for-you" vegetables.

5 The wonderful _____ of our tomato sauce will make your mouth water.

6 Special offer! Order a _____ with your pizza, and we'll refill your glass for free.

7 We want you to get enough to eat, but please don't be a _____.

8 Try our favorite topping. It's _____ chunks of tender chicken.

9 A meal at Peppy's is like going to a _____ at a palace.

10 Once you've tried one of Peppy's pizzas, you'll be back. That's because you'll _____ another one of his pizzas soon.

Name _____   Date _____

Discover the Hidden Words

Directions: Write the correct vocabulary word next to each definition. Then, to find the hidden word, write each numbered letter from your answers on the matching numbered line near the bottom of the page.

a a large and very fancy meal

— — — —
        3

b describing healthy food that's good for the body

— — — — — — — — —
9

c a nice scent or smell

— — — — —
        5

d a liquid that people drink

— — — — — — — —
            7

e to wish for or desire very much

— — — — —
    1

f a greedy person who eats too much

— — — — — — —
            10

g to eat very hungrily and completely

— — — — — —
          6

h able to be eaten

— — — — — —
            2

i very hungry

— — — — — —
    8

j very pleasing to taste

— — — — — — — —
          4

The hidden word is:

— — — — — — — — — —
1   2   3   4   5   6   7   8   9   10

Are You a Word Whiz?

What do you think the word "famine" means? Take a guess and then look it up in a dictionary to see if you're right.

My guess: _____

Name _____ Date _____

Get to Know Some High-Energy Hiking Words!

On their summer vacation, Steve and his family hiked to the top of a mountain. It was awesome! Here are some of the words that Steve used when he described this climb in his travel journal.

Directions: To help you recall what these vocabulary words mean, draw pictures or write words in each box.

apparel – (n.) things that are worn by a person

hazardous – (adj.) full of danger

barren – (adj.) not fruitful or producing much, without plant growth

obstacle – (n.) something that prevents forward movement

encounter – (v.) to come upon unexpectedly, to be faced with

provisions – (n.) supplies, particularly food and drinks

essential – (adj.) needed, very important

stamina – (n.) the ability to keep doing something without getting tired

exuberant – (adj.) filled with joy and happiness

summit – (n.) the highest point, usually the top of a mountain

Memory Boosters

1. The word *provide* means "to make available or supply what is needed." Which of these words is related to the word *provide*? _____

2. If something is bare, it is plain, empty, or without covering. Which of these words is related to the word *bare*? _____

3. What memory boosters can you think up to help you remember the words in this vocabulary packet? Write your ideas next to the words or on a separate sheet of paper.

Name _____   Date _____

Synonym Match

Directions: Draw a line from each word in the left column to its synonym in the right column.
Remember: a synonym is a word that has the same or nearly the same meaning.

1	exuberant	peak
2	stamina	clothing
3	provisions	meet
4	summit	necessary
5	hazardous	excited
6	apparel	empty
7	barren	barrier
8	encounter	energy
9	obstacle	supplies
10	essential	risky

What Do You Think?

Directions: List your ideas for each prompt.

Here are four things that I would include in my **provisions** for an overnight camping trip.

_____   _____

_____   _____

These are two things that are **essential** to do each day.

_____   _____

Here are two things that make me feel **exuberant**.

_____   _____

Name _____   Date _____

Which Fits Best?

Directions: Fill in the blanks with one of the vocabulary words. Use each word just once.

obstacle(s)	summit	hazardous	apparel	barren
exuberant	essential	stamina	encounter(ed)	provisions

My Travel Journal

July 16

Today was one of the best days of our trip. We climbed to the very top of a mountain! First we stopped at the ranger station to get a trail map and advice for our climb. The ranger was very helpful and told us it was _____ to have warm _____,
(1)   (2)
since it might be quite windy and cold near the peak. She also suggested that we take adequate _____, such as drinking water, snacks for the trail, and a first-aid kit.
(3)

At first the trail was fairly flat, but it quickly became steeper and more rocky. In some places the trail was wet and slippery, making our climb more _____. We
(4)
_____ several _____, including a large tree
(5)   (6)
that had fallen across the trail and a wide patch of mud that we had to step around carefully so we wouldn't lose our footing!

As we neared the _____, the land became quite
(7)
_____. There were no trees, just patches of snow. My energy was
(8)
beginning to fade, and the trail was getting even steeper. I began to wonder if I had enough _____ to make it all the way to the top. My sister convinced me that I
(9)
could do it, and with one last burst of strength I made it.

The view was amazing. We could see other mountains all around us, even the ranger station where we had begun our hike. It looked so tiny from up there on the mountain top. Having made it all the way, I was _____! The whole way down, I felt very
(10)
proud of myself!

Name _____   Date _____

Discover the Hidden Words

Directions: Write the correct vocabulary word next to each definition. Then, to find the hidden answer, write each numbered letter from your answers on the matching numbered line at the bottom.

a bubbling over with happiness

_ _ _ _ _ _ _ _
          6

b with nothing growing

_ _ _ _ _ _
        10

c the top of a mountain

_ _ _ _ _ _
  3   12

d very needed

_ _ _ _ _ _ _ _
        5

e shirts, sweaters, and pants, for example

_ _ _ _ _ _
      9

f an antonym for "safe"

_ _ _ _ _ _ _ _
              11

g the physical strength to keep going

_ _ _ _ _ _ _
      1

h food and drinks for a hike

_ _ _ _ _ _ _ _ _
    2 7

i something that blocks the way

_ _ _ _ _ _ _ _
              8

j to come upon by chance

_ _ _ _ _ _ _ _
  4

The world's tallest mountain is:

___ ___ ___ ___ ___   ___ ___ ___ ___ ___ ___ ___
 1   2   3   4   5   6   7   8   9 10 11 12

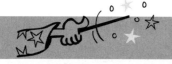

Are You a Word Whiz?

The elevation of the world's tallest mountain is over 29,000 feet. What do you think *elevation* means? Take a guess and then look it up in a dictionary to see if you're right.

My guess: _____

Instant Homework Packets: Vocabulary © 2010 by Jan Meyer. Scholastic Teaching Resources

Homework
Packet #13

What's So
Funny, Tucker
Tickle?

Page 1

Name _____   Date _____

Get to Know Some Rib-Tickling Words!

I get a kick out of my own shenanigans!

Tucker Tickle is amused by synonyms for *funny.* He is also entertained by words that look funny or sound funny. These are some of his favorites.

Directions: To help you recall what these vocabulary words mean, draw pictures or write words in each box.

bamboozle – (v.) to trick or mislead	**knickknack** – (n.) a small, ornamental object of little value
cantankerous – (adj.) ill-tempered, irritable	**rambunctious** – (adj.) noisy and wild, disorderly
chortle – (v.) to chuckle or snort with amusement	**scalawag** – (n.) a rascal, someone who plays pranks on others
dillydally – (v.) to put off what one should be doing, to dawdle	**shenanigans** – (n.) playful trickery, nonsense
hubbub – (n.) a loud, confused noise	**skedaddle** – (n.) to run away in a hurry

Memory Boosters

1. The word *ram* can mean "to push hard." Which of these words starts with the word *ram*? _____

2. The word *delay* can mean to "act later than expected" or to "put off." Which of these words has two words joined together—each of which (like *delay*) starts with a *d*, ends with a *y* and has an *l* in the middle? _____

3. What memory boosters can you think up to help you remember the words in this vocabulary packet? Write your ideas next to the words or on a separate sheet of paper.

Name _____   Date _____

Same or Different?

Directions: Each of the pairs of words below are antonyms or synonyms. If the words are antonyms (opposite in meaning), circle "A." If the words are synonyms (the same or similar in meaning), circle "S."

1 knickknack   decoration   A   S

2 rambunctious quiet   A   S

3 chortle   sob   A   S

4 cantankerous cranky   A   S

5 shenanigans   pranks   A   S

6 hubbub   uproar   A   S

7 bamboozle   fool   A   S

8 skedaddle   depart   A   S

9 scalawag   trickster   A   S

10 dillydally   hurry   A   S

What Do You Think?

Directions: List your ideas for each prompt.

Here are two times when I might want to **dillydally**.

_____

_____

This is something that a **scalawag** might do.

_____

Here are three things that would make me **chortle**.

_____

_____

_____

56

Name _____   Date _____

Which Fits Best?

Directions: Fill in the blanks with one of the vocabulary words. Use each word just once.

hubbub	chortle(d)	bamboozle(d)	scalawag	rambunctious
knickknack(s)	cantankerous	skedaddle(d)	shenanigans	dillydally

That's Ridiculous

1   Sylvester Sly _____ a foolish man into buying a car without an engine.

2   There was a great _____ when the helicopter made an emergency landing in the middle of a large playground.

3   Nellie screamed when her little brother's wind-up mouse ran across the kitchen floor. "Stop your _____," Nellie said crossly to her brother.

4   When some young Halloween trick-or-treaters came to his door, the _____old man shook his fist and shouted, "Go away!"

5   The frog said to the snail, "If you don't _____, I'm sure you'll win the race against the beetle."

6   The _____ put a big rubber spider on top of the birthday cake.

7   Mrs. McBoodle has a collection of 50 little china poodles. She keeps these _____ on top of a pink table in her living room.

8   The _____ crowd pushed and shoved to get a better view of the 100-pound turkey in the Thanksgiving Day parade.

9   Wilma the witch _____ on her broomstick when a black cat began to chase her.

10   Chester Chumm _____ when he saw a chubby chimp chewing a chunky chocolate chip cookie.

Name _____ Date _____

Discover the Hidden Words

Directions: Write the correct vocabulary word next to each definition. Then, to find the hidden answer to the riddle, write each numbered letter from your answers on the matching numbered line at the bottom. **Riddle:** What should you do if your toe falls off?

a decorative object bought at a small cost _ _ _ _ _ _ _ _
                                                         2

b to cheat or fool someone _ _ _ _ _ _ _
                                      7

c noisy confusion _ _ _ _ _ _
                          11

d to rush off _ _ _ _ _ _ _
                          4

e to waste time _ _ _ _ _ _
                      3

f to laugh with joy _ _ _ _ _
                      1

g loud and disorderly _ _ _ _ _ _ _ _ _
                        10   6

h silly pranks _ _ _ _ _ _ _
                      5

i disagreeable, cross _ _ _ _ _ _ _
                            9   13

j someone who likes to play tricks _ _ _ _ _ _
                                      12   8

The answer is:

_ _ _ _ _ _ _ _ _ _ _ _ _
1 2 3 4 5 6 7 8 9 10 11 12 13

Are You a Word Whiz?

Hilarious is a synonym that Tucker Tickle really likes. What do you think the word *hilarious* means? Take a guess and then look it up in a dictionary to see if you're right.

My guess: _____

Name _____ Date _____

Get to Know Some Words That Are Commonly Confused!

I assent to asscend the mountain and rescue the prince.

Already and *all ready* are often confused. *Already* means "by this time" or "before this time." *All ready* means "totally prepared." Here are five word pairs that are commonly confused.

Directions: To help you recall what these vocabulary words mean, draw pictures or write words in each box.

☐	**adapt** – (v.) to adjust or fix to fit a new situation	☐	**commend** – (v.) to speak well of
☐	**adept** – (adj.) skillful, expert	☐	**device** – (n.) something used to do a job—a tool or piece of equipment, for example
☐	**ascend** – (v.) to go up or climb	☐	**devise** – (v.) to make a plan, invent or develop
☐	**assent** – (v.) to agree or consent	☐	**precede** – (v.) to go or come before in order, place, or time
☐	**commence** – (v.) to make a start	☐	**proceed** – (v.) to go on, especially after stopping

💡 Memory Boosters

1 The prefix *pre-* means "before." Which of these words starts with the prefix *pre-*?
_____

2 An ice pick is a tool that is used to break up ice. Which of these words ends with the word *ice*? _____

3 What memory boosters can you think up to help you remember the words in this vocabulary packet? Write your ideas next to the words or on a separate sheet of paper.

Name _____ Date _____

Same or Different?

Directions: Each of the pairs of words below are antonyms or synonyms. If the words are antonyms (opposite in meaning), circle "A." If the words are synonyms (the same or similar in meaning), circle "S."

1	devise	create	A	S	6	adept	unskilled	A	S
2	ascend	rise	A	S	7	commence	end	A	S
3	proceed	stop	A	S	8	precede	follow	A	S
4	adapt	adjust	A	S	9	commend	praise	A	S
5	device	tool	A	S	10	assent	disagree	A	S

What Do You Think?

Directions: List your ideas for each prompt.

Here are four small but useful **devices** you can find in a kitchen.

_____   _____

_____   _____

These are two things at which I am **adept**.

_____   _____

_____   _____

Here are the two months that **precede** July.

_____   _____

Name _____ Date _____

Which Fits Best?

Directions: Fill in the blanks with the correct word
from each pair of commonly confused words.

assent   ascend

All Right! I Bet You
Get These All Right

All right can mean both "yes" and "without any errors."
Alright is not a formally accepted spelling.

---

1 Luis had to _____ a ladder to get to his tree house.
(**assent** or **ascend**)

2 Carla hopes that her parents will _____ to let her visit her friend's
(**assent** or **ascend**)

lake house.

3 Josh wants to _____ a _____ that will help him
(**device** or **devise**)   (**device** or **devise**)

get up on time on schooldays. He's thinking about a mechanical arm that comes out from his

alarm clock.

4 Everyone _____ Angelo on the speech that he made.
(**commend(ed)** or **commence(d)**)

5 Summer camp _____ on July 12.
(**commend(ed)** or **commence(d)**)

6 The soccer game will _____ as soon as it stops raining.
(**proceed** or **precede**)

7 "If we line up alphabetically, Aaron and Aisha will _____ me," said Alex.
(**proceed** or **precede**)

8 When Marissa's family moved from a small town to San Francisco, she had to

_____ to living in a big city.
(**adept** or **adapt**)

9 Erik is an _____ ice skater. He can do figure eights and amazing spins.
(**adept** or **adapt**)

Name _____   Date _____

Crossword Craze

Directions: Complete this crossword puzzle by filling in the vocabulary words that fit the definitions.

Across

3 to make fit for a different purpose

5 to begin

7 to create

8 using a staircase, for example

9 to give one's consent to

Down

1 to praise someone

2 to move forward

3 expert at something

4 to go in front of

6 something created for a special use

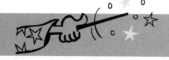

Are You a Word Whiz?

The words *except* and *accept* are often confused. Which of these words means "besides" or "in stead of"? Take a guess and then look it up in a dictionary to see if you're right.

My guess: _____

Homework
Packet #15
From Honking
Geese to Honking
Horns
Page 1

Name _____   Date _____

Get to Know Some City and Country Words!

Akiko and her family moved from a farm in the country to New York City. "I miss the country, but the city is exciting!" Akiko says. Here are some words she uses to describe country and city life.

Directions: To help you recall what these vocabulary words mean, draw pictures or write words in each box.

graze – (v.) to feed on growing grass	**pasture** – (n.) a grassy field where animals can feed
hectic – (adj.) full of busy activity and confusion	**picturesque** – (adj.) pleasing or charming to look at
illuminated – (adj.) supplied with light	**populous** – (adj.) full of people
numerous – (adj.) a great quantity, very many	**rural** – (adj.) of or related to the country
orchard – (n.) a place where fruit trees are planted and grow	**urban** – (adj.) having to do with cities

💡 Memory Boosters

1 *Population* refers to the number of people in a place. Which of these words means a large number of people in a place? _____

2 One of the meanings of *number* is "quantity, especially a large number." Which of these words is related to *number*? _____

3 What memory boosters can you think up to help you remember the words in this vocabulary packet? Write your ideas next to the words or on a separate sheet of paper.

Homework
Packet #15

From Honking
Geese to Honking
Horns
Page 2

Name _____ Date _____

Which Is Which?

Directions: Write each vocabulary word that relates to the country in the oval on the left. Write each vocabulary word that relates to the city in the oval on the right. If you think that a word relates to both the city and the country, write it in the area where the shapes overlap.

orchard	pasture	illuminated	urban	graze
numerous	hectic	rural	populous	picturesque

Country   City

What Do You Think?

Directions: List your ideas for each prompt.

Here are three things that could be picked from trees in an **orchard**.

_____   _____

_____

These are two animals that **graze**.

_____   _____

Here are two places that I think are **picturesque**.

_____   _____

Homework
Packet #15
From Honking
Geese to Honking
Horns
Page 3

Name _____   Date _____

Which Fits Best?

Directions: Fill in the blanks with one of the vocabulary words. Use each word just once.

orchard	pasture	illuminated	urban	graze
numerous	hectic	rural	populous	picturesque

Dear Grandma,

Life in a city is not at all like life in a _____ (1) area. I miss climbing trees in

our _____ (2) and being able to pick apples there in the fall. Now Mom and I will

have to pick our apples in the fruit section at the supermarket. I miss our sheep, too. I liked to watch

them _____ (3) in the _____ (4). Sheep are so cute! Most of all,

I miss Honker, my pet goose. I have a picture of him on my dresser so I won't forget him.

As you know, there were ponds, fields of sunflowers, and pretty stone fences near our farm

in the country. It was so very _____ (5)! My views are quite different now. I like

looking at the _____ (6) tall buildings and visiting Times Square. That's an area

that's filled with theaters, all sorts of restaurants, and lots of colorful _____ (7) signs.

_____ (8) life can be pretty _____ (9).

Streets are filled with buses, cars, and taxis. Sidewalks are filled with crowds of people. That's

particularly true here in New York because it is the most _____ (10) city in the

United States.

When you come to visit at Thanksgiving, we'll go to museums, the Statue of Liberty, and take

rides on the subway. There's so much to do here! I think I'm glad we moved.

Love,

Akiko

Name _____   Date _____

Discover the Hidden Words

Directions: Write the correct vocabulary word next to each definition. Then, to find the hidden message, write each numbered letter from your answers on the matching numbered line near the bottom of the page.

a   a field of growing grass where animals can feed

— — — — — —
12   1   14

b   the opposite of "urban"

— — — — —
          18

c   describing a place with many people

— — — — — — — —
6   10

d   the opposite of "unlit"

— — — — — — — —
7   5

e   a place where you might pick cherries

— — — — — — —
      2   19

f   the opposite of "calm"

— — — — — —
    9   13 17

g   the opposite of "ugly"

— — — — — — — —
  20 11   3

h   what a cow might do in a grassy field

— — — — —
22   4

i   having to do with cities

— — — —
16 15

j   the opposite of "very few"

— — — — — — —
21   8

One of Akiko's favorite New York City sights is:

__ __ __ __ __ __ __ __ __
1   2   3   4   5   6   7   8   9

__ __ __ __ __ __ __ __ __ __ __ __ __
10 11 12 13 14 15 16 17 18 19 20 21 22

Are You a Word Whiz?

Another city word is *skyscraper.* What do you think a *skyscraper* is? Take a guess and then look it up in a dictionary to see if you're right.

My guess: _____

Instant Homework Packets: Vocabulary © 2010 by Jan Meyer. Scholastic Teaching Resources

Name _____   Date _____

Get to Know Some Olympian Words!

The first Olympic Games took place in ancient Greece. Then, winners wore olive wreaths on their heads. Today, winners receive gold, silver, or bronze medals. Here are some words that have to do with the Olympics.

Directions: To help you recall what these vocabulary words mean, draw pictures or write words in each box.

☐	**achievement** – (n.) something gained or won by special effort
☐	**arduous** – (adj.) very hard to do, very difficult
☐	**champion** - (n.) someone who wins first place in a contest or game
☐	**debut** – (n.) a first public appearance
☐	**flawless** – (adj.) without a mistake or fault

☐	**extraordinary** – (adj.) very unusual, beyond what is ordinary
☐	**procession** - (n.) a group of people moving forward together in an orderly line
☐	**spectator** – (n.) someone who looks at something without taking part
☐	**structure** – (n.) something that has been built
☐	**symbol** – (n.) something that stands for an idea

Memory Boosters

1 The word *construct* means "to build something." Which of these words has the word part *struct* in it? _____

2 Which word means "very hard" and has a beginning that sounds like "hard"?

_____

3 What memory boosters can you think up to help you remember the words in this vocabulary packet? Write your ideas next to the words or on a separate sheet of paper.

Name _____ Date _____

Synonym Match

Directions: Draw a line from each word in the left column to its synonym in the right column. Remember: a synonym is a word that has the same or nearly the same meaning.

1	structure	success
2	champion	watcher
3	debut	parade
4	extraordinary	perfect
5	spectator	difficult
6	symbol	building
7	arduous	introduction
8	procession	winner
9	achievement	representation
10	flawless	special

What Do You Think?

Directions: List your ideas for each prompt.

Here are two things at which I have been a **spectator.**

_____   _____

These are two **achievements** of which I am very proud.

_____   _____

Here is something that I think is **arduous.**

_____

Instant Homework Packets: Vocabulary © 2010 by Jan Meyer. Scholastic Teaching Resources

Name _____ Date _____

Which Fits Best?

Directions: Fill in the blanks with one of the vocabulary words. Use each word just once.

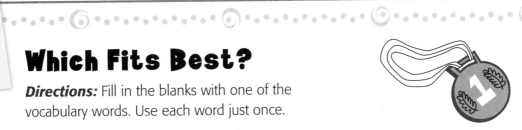

| structure(s) | champion | achievement | arduous | flawless |
| debut | procession | symbol | extraordinary | spectator(s) |

The Olympics

The Olympic Games begin with a special program that includes _____

(1)

entertainment, the lighting of the Olympic flame, and a _____ of the athletes,

(2)

who have come from all over the world to take part in the sports events.

The _____ for the Olympics is five colored rings. These rings are linked to

(3)

represent the Olympic spirit of friendship.

The host cities often build new _____ for the Olympic events. In Sydney,

(4)

Australia, a new stadium with seating for more than 10,000 _____ was built for

(5)

the 2000 Summer Olympics.

To prepare for the Olympics, athletes must follow a/an _____,

(6)

long-term training program.

The Summer Olympics now has over 300 different events. In 2004, women's wrestling made its

_____. Figure skating is an exciting event to watch during the Winter Olympics.

(7)

To win a gold medal, a figure skater's performance must be as _____ as

(8)

possible.

At the 1976 Summer Olympics, Nadia Comaneci, a 14-year old girl from Romania,

became the first gymnast to be awarded a perfect score by the judges. That was an outstanding

_____. At the 2008 Summer Olympics, Michael Phelps, an American swimmer,

(9)

became the first Olympic _____ to win eight gold medals in one Olympics.

(10)

Name _____

Date _____

Discover the Hidden Words

Directions: Write the correct vocabulary word next to each definition. Then, to find the hidden answer, write each numbered letter from your answers on the matching numbered line at the bottom.

Question: What Olympic event combines three different sports—swimming, cycling, and running?

a   something done that requires skill or effort
— — — — — — — — — —
             9

b   the first time something is seen publicly
— — — — —
             4

c   the opposite of "filled with mistakes"
— — — — — — —
             10

d   people moving forward in a formal manner
— — — — — — — — — —
                             12

e   the winner of a gold medal in the Olympics
— — — — — — —
 2 7

f   something that represents something else
— — — — — —
             11

g   a person who watches an activity
— — — — — — — —
   3

h   requiring much effort
— — — — — —
 5

i   very remarkable
— — — — — — — — — — —
                       6

j   a house, hotel, or garage
— — — — — — — —
 8   1

The name of the event is:

— — —   — — — — — — — — — —
1 2 3   4 5 6 7 8 9 10 11 12

Are You a Word Whiz?

The word *flawless* ends with the suffix *-less*. What do you think the suffix *-less* means? Take a guess and then look it up in a dictionary to see if you're right.

My guess: _____

Name _____   Date _____

Get to Know Some Amazing Art Words!

Pablo Pescado is a famous artist who makes beautiful "word paintings." In one painting, he formed the letters in the word "jungle" using vines, snakes, and butterflies. Here are words for his next ten paintings.

Directions: To help you recall what these vocabulary words mean, draw pictures or write words in each box.

☐	**excel** – (v.) to be outstanding or superior, at something	☐	**landscape** – (n.) a picture showing a scene on land
☐	**exhibit** – (v.) to show or display in public	☐	**masterpiece** – (n) one of the best works by an artist
☐	**figure** – (n.) a representation of a person in a picture or drawing	☐	**portrait** – (adj.) a painting, a drawing, or a photograph of a person, especially of the face
☐	**hue** – (adj.) a shade or tone of a color	☐	**realistic** – (adj.) like the real thing
☐	**ingenious** – (adj.) showing cleverness, originality, and imagination	☐	**vivid** – (adj.) very bright or lively

Memory Boosters

1 The word *excellent* means "outstanding" or "extremely good." Which of these words is spelled with the first five letters of *excellent*? _____

2 The word *real* means "actual" or "true." Which of these words is a form of the word *real*? _____

3 What memory boosters can you think up to help you remember the words in this vocabulary packet? Write your ideas next to the words or on a separate sheet of paper.

Same or Different?

Directions: Each of the pairs of words below are antonyms or synonyms. If the words are antonyms (opposite in meaning), circle "A." If the words are synonyms (the same or similar in meaning), circle "S."

1	masterpiece	scribble	A S	6	excel	fail	A S
2	hue	shade	A S	7	figure	person	A S
3	exhibit	hide	A S	8	realistic	imaginary	A S
4	landscape	scene	A S	9	portrait	likeness	A S
5	vivid	dull	A S	10	ingenious	clever	A S

My Art Work

Directions: Sketch a portrait and a landscape to show the difference.

Here is a portrait.

Here is a landscape.

Title _____

Title _____

Name _____   Date _____

Which Fits Best?

Directions: Fill in the blanks with one of the vocabulary words. Use each word just once.

| exhibit(ed) | masterpiece(s) | vivid | hue(s) | realistic |
| landscape(s) | excel(led) | portrait(s) | ingenious | figure(s) |

My Life as a Painter
by Pablo Pescado

It was no surprise to my parents that I have become an important artist. Even as a

very young child I _____ in art. I liked to draw houses, trees, and stick
(1)

_____. While I was in art school, I began painting _____
(2)   (3)

of my sister. At first my teachers were shocked because in some of these pictures I gave my sister

three eyes. In others, she has an ear where her nose should be. Soon, though, they decided that these

paintings were exciting and _____.
(4)

When I was only twenty-five, a large group of my paintings were _____ at
(5)

a popular art gallery in Los Angeles. By then, I was painting _____ of the woods
(6)

and fields near my home. I used _____ reds, pinks, and purples for the trees
(7)

and different _____ of green or yellow for the sky. Although some people were
(8)

upset that the colors weren't _____, most people loved these pictures and paid
(9)

thousands of dollars for them.

Now I have started something new. It is a series of what I call "word paintings." Happily,

museums and art collectors are already interested in buying them. In fact, a

few of these paintings are being called _____.
(10)

Name _____   Date _____

Discover the Hidden Words

Directions: Write the correct vocabulary word next to each definition. Then, to find the hidden message, write each numbered letter from your answers on the matching numbered line near the bottom of the page.

a   a picture of a person   __ __ __ __ __ __ __ __
                                         10

b   an artist's best work   __ __ __ __ __ __ __ __ __ __
                                    16   11

c   shade or tint of a color   __ __ __ __
                                  1

d   inventive, original   __ __ __ __ __ __ __ __
                                     8   7

e   a picture of a land scene __ __ __ __ __ __ __ __ __
                                     14   3

f   display in a public place __ __ __ __ __ __ __
                                        13   15

g   true to life   __ __ __ __ __ __ __
                                     12   2

h   to do better than others   __ __ __ __ __
                                        9

i   brilliantly colored   __ __ __ __ __
                                  6   4

j   a person in a drawing   __ __ __ __ __ __
                                5

For my very first painting I

__ __ __ __   __ __ __ __ __ __
1 2 3 4   5 6 7 8 9 10

__ __ __ __ __ __ .
11 12 13 14 15 16

Are You a Word Whiz?

What do you think a *self-portrait* is? Take a guess and then look it up in a dictionary to see if you're right.

My guess: _____

Name _____ Date _____

Homework Packet #18

It Takes All Kinds

Page 1

Get to Know Some Pertinent Personality Words!

Mrs. Peterson teaches fifth grade. What she loves best about her students is that each one is unique. Here are ten different words that describe ten of her students.

Directions: To help you recall what these vocabulary words mean, draw pictures or write words in each box.

| | Energetic Emma |

ambitious – (adj.) filled with a desire to be a success

confident – (adj.) sure of oneself and one's abilities

courteous – (adj.) thoughtful of others, showing good manners

energetic – (adj.) full of energy, active

entertaining – (adj.) interesting, amusing, enjoyable to be with

inquisitive – (adj.) eager to find out about things

mischievous – (adj.) full of pranks and teasing fun

patient – (adj.) having a willingness to wait

sensible – (adj.) showing good sense and judgment

sociable – (adj.) enjoying company, friendly

Memory Boosters

1. A quiz is a short test that asks questions. Which of these words has a second syllable that sounds like *quiz*? _____

2. If something makes sense, it is reasonable or a good idea. Which of these words has most of the word *sense* in it? _____

3. What memory boosters can you think up to help you remember the words in this vocabulary packet? Write your ideas next to the words or on a separate sheet of paper.

Instant Homework Packets: Vocabulary © 2010 by Jan Meyer. Scholastic Teaching Resources

75

Name _____   Date _____

Same or Different?

Directions: Each of the pairs of words below are antonyms or synonyms. If the words are antonyms (opposite in meaning), circle "A." If the words are synonyms (the same or similar in meaning), circle "S."

1 entertaining   boring   A   S   6   inquisitive   curious   A   S

2 sociable   friendly   A   S   7   sensible   foolish   A   S

3 ambitious   lazy   A   S   8   courteous   rude   A   S

4 confident   sure   A   S   9   mischievous   serious   A   S

5 energetic   peppy   A   S   10 patient   impatient   A   S

 # What Do You Think?

Directions: List your ideas for each prompt.

These are two things that I have done that were **courteous**.

_____

_____

Here are two things about which I am **confident**.

_____

_____

These are two things that I think are **entertaining**.

_____   _____

Name _____   Date _____

Which Fits Best?

Directions: Fill in the blanks with one of the
vocabulary words. Use each word just once.

courteous	energetic	mischievous	patient	sociable
inquisitive	confident	ambitious	entertaining	sensible

Some of the Students in Mrs. Peterson's Class

1 Julia is very _____. She has lots of friends and likes to spend as much time as possible with them. She loves slumber parties and sending e-mails.

2 Gordon is very _____. He has big plans for his future. He wants to be an important scientist and is already reading books about science and scientists whenever he has time.

3 Leila is very _____. She likes to find out why things happen and how things work. She often searches for information in encyclopedias and on the Internet.

4 Wendy is playfully _____. She likes to think up silly pranks and loves to have fun on April Fools' Day.

5 Kareem is almost always very _____. He takes an umbrella when it looks like it might rain and does his homework right after school when there's something special he wants to do in the evening.

6 Adam is very _____. He always offers to help his mother carry heavy packages and often holds doors open for others.

7 Midori is very _____. She believes that she will do well at almost anything she tries to do.

8 Mario is very _____. He is fun to be with because he knows lots of jokes, riddles, spooky stories, and games to play.

9 Doug is very _____. He never seems to get tired. He walks to and from school even though he could ride the bus.

10 Keesha is very _____. She never pushes in front of others and always waits quietly for her turn.

Name _____   Date _____

Discover the Hidden Words

Directions: Write the correct vocabulary word next to each definition. Then, to find the hidden answer to the riddle, write each numbered letter from your answers on the matching numbered line at the bottom.

Riddle: When did Benjamin Franklin discover electricity?

a able to wait without complaining   __ __ __ __ __ __ __
                                            4

b full of questions   __ __ __ __ __ __ __ __ __
                        11   14

c enjoys doing playful teasing   __ __ __ __ __ __ __ __
                                   17   15

d enjoying being and doing things with others   __ __ __ __ __ __
                                                  13   7

e doing things that are wise to do   __ __ __ __ __ __ __
                                           5

f lively and active   __ __ __ __ __ __
                             16 6

g eager to do well   __ __ __ __ __ __ __
                       10 8

h fun to be around   __ __ __ __ __ __ __ __ __ __
                                3   12

i feeling one will do well   __ __ __ __ __ __ __
                                         1

j polite and thoughtful   __ __ __ __ __ __ __ __
                                9   2

The answer is:

__ __ __ __ __ __ __
1 2 3 4 5 6 7

__ __ __ __ __ __ __ __ __ __
8 9 10 11 12 13 14 15 16 17

Are You a Word Whiz?

What do you think the word *inquire* means? Take a guess and then look it up in a dictionary to see if you're right.

My guess: _____

Instant Homework Packets: Vocabulary © 2010 by Jan Meyer. Scholastic Teaching Resources

Name _____   Date _____

Get to Know Some
Scintillating Sleuthing Words!

Sleuth is a synonym for the word "detective." And that's exactly what Speedwell Smart is. Here are some of the words that Speedwell uses when he talks about the cases he's solved.

Directions: To help you recall what these vocabulary words mean, draw pictures or write words in each box.

accomplice – (n.) someone who helps another do a wrong or illegal act	**flee** – (v.) to get away by running
apprehend – (v.) to arrest a person	**investigation** – (n.) a close look into something
culprit – (n.) a person guilty of a crime or of doing something wrong	**perplexed** – (adj.) confused about something
cunning – (adj.) skilled at fooling people	**pursue** – (v.) to chase after in order to catch someone
disguise – (n.) clothes and actions used to hide one's identity	**thwart** – (v.) to prevent someone from doing something

Memory Boosters

1. The words *flee* and *flea* are homophones. (Homophones are words that sound the same but have different spellings and meanings.) If a dog is about to be attacked by fleas, what should it do?

   _____

2. The word *accompany* means "to go in company with." Which of these words starts with the first six letters of *accompany*? _____

3. What memory boosters can you think up to help you remember the words in this vocabulary packet? Write your ideas next to the words or on a separate sheet of paper.

Name _____   Date _____

Synonym Match

Directions: Draw a line from each word in the left column to its synonym in the right column. Remember: a synonym is a word that has the same or nearly the same meaning.

1	pursue	costume
2	culprit	run off
3	cunning	follow
4	apprehend	stop
5	disguise	examination
6	thwart	partner in crime
7	perplexed	wrongdoer
8	investigation	capture
9	flee	puzzled
10	accomplice	sly

What Do You Think?

Directions: List your ideas for each prompt.

Here are four mammals, insects, and/or reptiles from which I would **flee**.

_____   _____

_____   _____

This is what I would put on if I wanted to wear a **disguise**.

_____

Here are two things or subjects I would like to **investigate**.

_____   _____

Name _____   Date _____

Which Fits Best?

Directions: Fill in the blanks with one of the
vocabulary words. Use each word just once.

flee	investigation	perplexed	cunning	apprehend
accomplice	disguise	culprit	pursue(d)	thwart(ed)

The Case of the Missing Words

The police asked Speedwell to help in their _____ (1). They wanted to find out

who was putting fish in the town swimming pool. Using clues he found around the pool, he was able

to solve the case and help the police _____ (2) the _____ (3).

Speedwell's fast action and sharp eyes _____ (4) the escape of a bank robber

and his _____ (5) who was driving the getaway car.

Speedwell wore a _____ (6) when he followed the person that he thought

was selling stolen puppies. The dognapper tried to _____ (7), but Speedwell

_____ (8) him. The detective jumped over a fence and grabbed the thief. Mrs.

Rosen was very grateful to Speedwell when he returned her stolen puppy to her.

Everyone in town was _____ (9). Who, they wondered, was pasting fake

mustaches on the statues in the park? Speedwell solved the mystery by hiding one night in the bushes

near the statues.

"Some crooks have been cheating people by selling worthless jewelry for high prices," Speedwell

told his friends. "They are _____ (10), but I have a plan for a trap that is sure to catch

them!"

Name _____ Date _____

Discover the Hidden Words

Directions: Write the correct vocabulary word next to each definition. Then, to find the hidden message, write each numbered letter from your answers on the matching numbered line near the bottom of the page.

a feeling confused   ___ ___ ___ ___ ___ ___ ___
                                                            6

b to nab or arrest someone   ___ ___ ___ ___ ___ ___ ___
                                                                        3

c to block something from happening   ___ ___ ___ ___ ___ ___
                                                                  11

d someone who is guilty of doing something wrong   ___ ___ ___ ___ ___ ___ ___
                                                                          8

e something used to change the look of a person   ___ ___ ___ ___ ___ ___ ___
                                                                          2

f to try to get away by hurrying away   ___ ___ ___ ___
                                                            1

g a careful search for information   ___ ___ ___ ___ ___ ___ ___ ___ ___ ___ ___
                                                            5   9

h a person who helps another in a crime   ___ ___ ___ ___ ___ ___ ___ ___ ___
                                                                        7

i clever at tricking others   ___ ___ ___ ___ ___ ___
                                                            10   4

j to follow in order to catch someone   ___ ___ ___ ___ ___ ___
                                                                  12

Speedwell Smart found

___ ___ ___ ___ ___ ___ ___ ___ ___ ___ ___ ___ .
 1   2   3   4   5   6   7   8   9   10 11 12

Are You a Word Whiz?

A culprit is culpable of doing something wrong. What do you think the word *culpable* means? Take a guess and then look it up in a dictionary to see if you're right.

My guess: _____

Name _____   Date _____

Get to Know Some Rain Forest Words!

Professor Flora Fowler is in a Central American rain forest to study the animal and plant life. Here are some of the words she has recorded in her field notebook.

Directions: To help you recall what these vocabulary words mean, draw pictures or write words in each box.

☐	**audible** – (adj.) loud enough to be heard	☐	**hover** – (v.) to remain in one place over an object or location
☐	**dense** – (adj.) tightly packed, close together	☐	**lethargic** – (adj.) slow moving, with a lack of energy
☐	**detect** – (v.) to discover something not easily seen or heard	☐	**solitary** – (adj.) without the company of others
☐	**flourish** – (v.) to develop or grow well	☐	**suspend** – (v.) to hang down by attaching to something above
☐	**foliage** – (n.) the leaves of a plant	☐	**vast** – (adj.) very large in area or amount

Memory Boosters

1 A detective is someone whose job is to discover information about something that is hard to figure out. Which of these words is found in the beginning of the word *detective*? _____

2 A *solo* is something done by oneself. Which of these words begins with the first three letters of *solo*? _____

3 What memory boosters can you think up to help you remember the words in this vocabulary packet? Write your ideas next to the words or on a separate sheet of paper.

Name _____   Date _____

Synonym Match

Directions: Draw a line from each word in the left column to its synonym in the right column. Remember: a synonym is a word that has the same or nearly the same meaning.

1	foliage	succeed
2	detect	inactive
3	dense	leaves
4	flourish	alone
5	suspend	huge
6	hover	float
7	lethargic	crowded
8	vast	hearable
9	audible	notice
10	solitary	hang

What Do You Think?

Directions: List your ideas for each prompt.

Here are two things that I might **detect** if I took a walk in the country, the woods, or a park.

_____   _____

These are two things that can be **solitary** activities.

_____   _____

Here are two things that are **audible** while I am doing this homework.

_____   _____

These are two things that are **vast**.

_____   _____

Name _____   Date _____

Which Fits Best?

Directions: Fill in the blanks with one of the vocabulary words. Use each word just once.

lethargic	suspend(ed)	solitary	detect	audible
vast	foliage	flourish	hover	dense

Field Notebook

It took sharp eyes for me to be able to _____ a three-toed sloth hanging in
(1)

the tree above me. At first, this animal looked like a huge, grey nest. The three-toed sloth hangs upside

down from tree branches, _____ by the curved, hooked claws at the ends of its
(2)

arms. This _____ animal is very slow moving, sleeps about 18 hours each day,
(3)

and comes down from its tree only about once a week.

The plant life is so _____ here that I feel like I am being closed
(4)

in by a wall of green _____, roots, and tree trunks. Feathery ferns
(5)

_____ here. That's because these plants grow well in places that are
(6)

warm and damp.

Each morning I hear the loud calls of the howler monkeys. Their howls are so loud that they are

_____ two or more miles away.
(7)

I am hoping to see a jaguar this evening. This _____ animal usually sets
(8)

out by itself to hunt when it grows dark.

Leafcutter ants are tireless workers. They cut up pieces of leaves with their scissor-like jaws.

Then, working together, they carry them back to their _____ underground nests.
(9)

Some nests have more than five million ants living in them.

Brightly colored hummingbirds are fun to watch as they _____ near
(10)

flowers, sucking up nectar with the long tongues in their beaks.

Name _____   Date _____

Reverse Crossword Puzzle

Directions: This crossword puzzle already has the words filled in. Your job is to come up with a definition, synonym, or clue* that fits each word going across or down. Then write them on the appropriate numbered lines below.

(*A clue for the word "hover," for example, might be "something a helicopter can do.")

```
                                             1
                                             f
                        2                    o
                        d                    l
        3          4                         i
        a  u  d  i  b  l  e                  i
                   e           7             a
    5         6    t     8   f               g
    h  o  v   e    e     s  o  l  i  t  a  r  y
          a        e        o                e
    9              t        u
    l  e  t  h  a  r  i  g  r  i  c
                            i
                            10
                            s  u  s  p  e  n  d
                            h
```

Across

3 _____

5 _____

8 _____

9 _____

10 _____

Down

1 _____

2 _____

4 _____

6 _____

7 _____

Are You a Word Whiz?

A tropical rain forest is warm throughout the year. This is because of its proximity to the equator. What do you think the word *proximity* means? Take a guess and then look it up in a dictionary to see if you're right.

My guess: _____

Word List

accomplice	79	confused	31	emerge	7
accumulate	43	conqueror	23	employer	23
achievement	67	conserve	15	encounter	51
acquire	19	convinced	7	endeavor	7
adapt	59	courteous	75	energetic	75
adept	59	crave	47	entertaining	75
agile	11	crucial	15	envious	19
ambitious	75	culprit	79	environment	15
apparel	51	cunning	79	essential	51
apprehend	79	cyclist	23	excel	73
apprehensive	27	debut	67	excessive	15
aquatic	11	delectable	47	exhibit	71
arduous	67	demonstrator	23	exterminator	23
aroma	47	dense	83	extinct	39
ascend	59	deserted	27	extraordinary	67
assent	59	detect	83	extravagant	19
astonishing	7	device	59	exuberant	51
audible	83	devise	59	famished	47
aviator	23	devour	47	feast	47
bamboozle	55	dilapidated	27	flawless	67
barren	51	dillydally	55	flee	79
beverage	47	diminish	43	flourish	83
blizzard	43	disappointed	31	figure	71
camouflage	39	disguise	79	foliage	83
cantankerous	55	disobedient	35	foolhardy	27
carnivore	39	displeased	35	frigid	43
celebrity	19	donation	19	fumes	15
champion	67	dreary	43	glutton	47
chortle	55	drench	43	grateful	31
commence	59	drizzle	43	graze	63
commend	59	edible	47	gusts	43
compete	11	eerie	27	habitat	39
conceal	7	elated	31	hazardous	51
confident	75	embarrassed	31	hectic	63

Word List

herbivore	39	obstacle	51	sociable	75
hibernate	39	offense	11	solitary	83
hover	83	opponent	11	spectator	67
hubbub	55	optimistic	31	stamina	51
hue	71	orchard	63	startle	27
humidity	43	pasture	63	stingy	19
illegal	35	patient	75	strenuous	11
illegible	35	perplexed	79	structure	67
illuminated	63	persistence	11	summit	51
immense	19	picturesque	63	supervisor	23
improbable	35	pollute	15	suspend	83
incapable	35	populous	63	sweltering	43
ingenious	71	portrait	71	symbol	67
inhabit	27	possessions	19	thwart	79
inquisitive	75	precede	59	tourist	23
interior	27	predator	39	tournament	11
interviewer	23	prey	39	toxic	15
investigation	79	proceed	59	tranquil	31
invisible	35	procession	67	trembling	27
irate	31	provisions	51	trophy	11
irreparable	35	pursue	79	unavailable	35
knickknack	55	rambunctious	55	uncomplicated	35
landscape	71	realistic	71	uneasy	31
lethargic	83	recycle	15	urban	63
litter	15	renowned	7	valuable	19
manicurist	23	reveal	7	vanish	7
masterpiece	71	rural	63	vast	83
migrate	39	rustle	27	vivid	71
mischievous	75	scalawag	55	wealthy	19
mystified	7	sensible	75	wilderness	15
nocturnal	39	shenanigans	55		
novice	11	skedaddle	55		
numerous	63	skeptical	7		
nutritious	47	sluggish	31		

Instant Homework Packets: Vocabulary © 2010 by Jan Meyer. Scholastic Teaching Resources

Word Card Template

Shapes for Counting Syllables

Count the number of syllables each vocabulary word has. Write the one-syllable words in the circle, the two-syllable words in the square, the three-syllable words in the triangle, and the four-syllable words in the octagon.

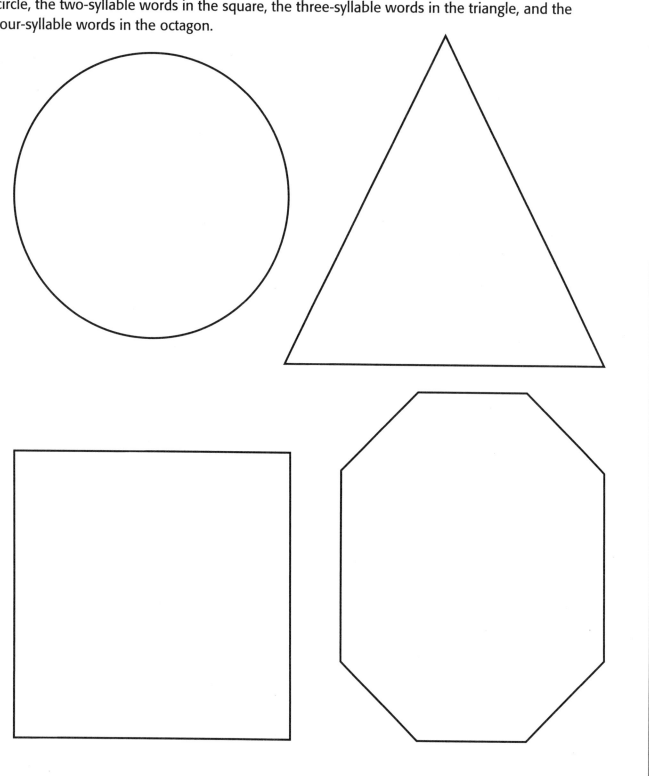

Instant Homework Packets: Vocabulary © 2010 by Jan Meyer. Scholastic Teaching Resources

Bonus Words

You may want to supplement the packet vocabulary word lists with these bonus words and incorporate them into some of the packet and reinforcement activities.

Wando the Wondrous
baffle
concentrate
disclose
awe
pretense
incredible

They're All Good Sports
strategy
vigorous
exert
participate
avid
victorious

Going Green
emission
negligent
deplete
compliance
receptacle
solar

Ritzy Mitzy's Million-Dollar Words
dazzle
profitable
exquisite
prosperous
luxurious
lavish

They're All People
adviser
pharmacist
invader
journalist
survivor
cartoonist

Shadowy Shapes and Ghostly Whispers
dread
stammer
cower
shrill
wary
desolate

Better Than Mad, Sad and Glad!
weary
content
exasperated
indignant
ashamed
alert

Lots of Nots
illiterate
irresponsible
discontinue
inadequate
insignificant
unimpressed

All About Animals
scurry
endangered
scavenger
pounce
burrow
species

Partly Cloudy and Warm
brisk
torrential
thaw
dismal
balmy
haze

Peppy Pepperoni's Food Favorites
hearty
banquet
morsel
portion
consume
nibble

To the Top
feat
terrain
precarious
vista
descend
crevice

Bonus Words

(Continued)

What's So Funny, Tucker Tickle?
rapscallion
snicker
hoodwink
hobnob
squeamish
garble

We're Already All Ready to Go
cease/seize
assure/insure
conscience/conscious

From Honking Geese to Honking Horns
dwell
harvest
rustic
pedestrian
congested
serene

Olympic Gold
ceremony
determination
contender
amateur
aspire
host

The Word Artist
inspiration
resemble
appeal
acclaim
sculpture
utilize

It Takes All Kinds
industrious
timid
reliable
dependable
considerate
competent

Speedwell Smart, Super Sleuth
bewilder
notorious
evade
skulk
suspicious
deter

A Rain Forest Expedition
plumage
diversity
abundance
lush
teem
incessant

Answer Key

WANDO THE WONDROUS
Page 7
1. conceal, reveal
2. mystified

Page 8
1. A 2. S 3. S 4. A 5. A
6. A 7. S 8. A 9. S 10. S
Answers will vary.

Page 9
1. renowned
2. skeptical
3. convinced
4. concealed
5. vanished
6. revealed
7. mystified
8. endeavor
9. emerged
10. astonishing

Page 10
a. convinced
b. renowned
c. reveal
d. skeptical
e. vanish
f. astonishing
g. mystified
h. conceal
i. emerge
j. endeavor
Answer: the floating piano

Word Whiz answers may vary. (Sample answer: something that has been revealed or made known)

THEY'RE ALL GOOD SPORTS
Page 11
1. opponent
2. strenuous

Page 12
1. A 2. S 3. A 4. A 5. S
6. S 7. A 8. A 9. A 10. A
Answers will vary.

Page 13
Denzel – offense
Kimberly – agile
Rosita – aquatic
Noah – novice
Ashley – trophy
Jason – strenuous
Tamika – opponent
Yoshi – compete
Jennifer – tournament
Kevin - persistence

Page 14
a. aquatic
b. novice
c. tournament
d. strenuous
e. opponent,
f. persistence
g. trophy
h. offense
i. agile
j. compete
Answer: It can catch flies.

Word Whiz answers may vary. (Sample answer: someone who explores underwater)

GOING GREEN
Page 15
1. recycle
2. wilderness

Page 16
1. S 2. A 3. S 4. A 5. A
6. S 7. S 8. S 9. A 10. A
Answers will vary.

Page 17
1. environment
2. toxic
3. recycle
4. conserve
5. excessive
6. crucial
7. wilderness
8. fumes
9. pollute
10. litter

Page 18
Answers will vary.
Word Whiz answers may vary. (Sample answer: poisons)

RITZY MITZY'S MILLION DOLLAR WORDS
Page 19
1. po$$e$$ion$
2. extravagant

Page 20
1. S 2. A 3. A 4. A 5. S
6. S 7. A 8. S 9. S 10. A
Answers will vary.

Page 21
1. celebrity
2. possessions
3. wealthy
4. immense
5. valuable
6. extravagant
7. acquired
8. envious
9. stingy
10. donations

Page 22
a. valuable
b. wealthy
c. immense
d. possessions
e. donation
f. stingy
g. celebrity
h. acquire
i. extravagant
j. envious
Answer: in a limousine

Word Whiz answers may vary. (Sample answer: something of which one gets ownership)

THEY'RE ALL PEOPLE
Page 23
1. interviewer
2. exterminator

Page 24
(-or) – demonstrate, aviate, conquer, supervise, exterminate
(-er) – interview, employ
(-ist) – manicure, cycle, tour
Answers will vary.

Page 25
1. tourists
2. conquerors
3. supervisor
4. cyclist
5. interviewer
6. employer
7. manicurist
8. demonstrator
9. aviator
10. exterminator

Page 26
a. exterminator
b. interviewer
c. employer
d. manicurist
e. demonstrator
f. cyclist
g. conqueror
h. tourist
i. supervisor
j. aviator
Answer: a contortionist

Word Whiz: guitarist

SHADOWY SHAPES AND GHOSTLY WHISPERS
Page 27
1. eerie
2. foolhardy

Page 28
1. A 2. S 3. A 4. A 5. S
6. A 7. S 8. A 9. A 10. A
Answers will vary.

Page 29
1. deserted
2. inhabited
3. dilapidated
4. apprehensive
5. foolhardy
6. eerie

7. rustle
8. interior
9. startled
10. trembling

Page 30
a. trembling
b. rustle
c. inhabit
d. eerie
e. foolhardy
f. dilapidated,
g. apprehensive
h. startle
i. deserted
j. interior
Answer: fasten your sheet belts

Word Whiz answers may vary. (Sample answer: the outside part of something)

BETTER THAN MAD, SAD, AND GLAD!
Page 31
1. sluggish
2. uneasy

Page 32
1. S 2. A 3. A 4. A 5. S
6. A 7. A 8. S 9. S 10. A
Answers will vary.

Page 33
1. irate
2. tranquil
3. confused
4. sluggish
5. embarrassed
6. grateful
7. elated
8. optimistic
9. uneasy
10. disappointed

Page 34
a. confused
b. embarrassed
c. tranquil
d. sluggish
e. elated
f. irate
g. uneasy

h. grateful
i. optimistic
j. disappointed
Answer: successful

Word Whiz answers may vary. (Sample answer: anger)

LOTS OF NOTS
Page 35
1. disobedient
2. incapable

Page 36
(il-) – legible, legal
(dis-) – obedient, pleased
(ir-) – reparable
(un-) – complicated, available
(im-) – probable
(in-) – capable, visible
Answers will vary.

Page 37
1. unavailable
2. uncomplicated
3. displeased
4. incapable
5. improbable
6. disobedient
7. illegal
8. irreparable
9. illegible
10. invisible

Page 38

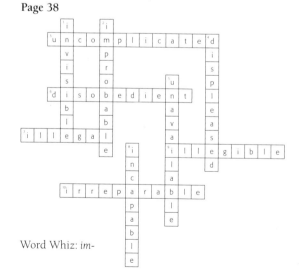

Word Whiz: *im-*

ALL ABOUT ANIMALS
Page 39
1. prey
2. habitat

Page 40
1. habitat
2. carnivore
3. predator
4. camouflage
5. nocturnal
6. herbivore
7. hibernate
Answers: an herbivore, prey, migrating

Page 41
1. migrates
2. habitat
3. herbivore
4. camouflage
5. predators
6. hibernate
7. carnivores
8. prey
9. nocturnal
10. extinct

Page 42
a. predator
b. migrate
c. carnivore
d. camouflage
e. prey
f. extinct

g. nocturnal
h. hibernate
i. habitat
j. herbivore
Answer: the giant anteater

Word Whiz answers may vary. (Sample answer: active during the day)

PARTLY CLOUDY AND WARM
Page 43
1. diminish
2. sweltering

Page 44
Circle – drench, gusts
Rectangle – blizzard, dreary, drizzle, frigid
Triangle – diminish, sweltering
Square – accumulate, humidity
Answers will vary.

Page 45
1. blizzard
2. accumulate
3. frigid
4. gusts
5. diminish
6. sweltering
7. humidity
8. dreary
9. drizzle
10. drenching

Page 46
Crossword answers will vary.

Word Whiz answers may vary. (Sample answer: to guess/and or announce what will happen ahead of time)

Instant Homework Packets: Vocabulary © 2010 by Jan Meyer. Scholastic Teaching Resources

**PEPPY PEPPERONI'S
FAVORITE WORDS**
Page 47
1. glutton
2. nutritious

Page 48
1. S 2. A 3. A 4. S 5. S
6. S 7. A 8. S 9. A 10. A
Answers will vary.

Page 49
1. famished
2. devour
3. edible
4. nutritious
5. aroma
6. beverage
7. glutton
8. delectable
9. feast
10. crave

Page 50
a. feast
b. nutritious
c. aroma
d. beverage
e. crave
f. glutton
g. devour
h. edible
i. famished
j. delectable
Answer: restaurant

Word Whiz answers may vary. (Sample answer: a period of hunger due to lack of food)

TO THE TOP
Page 51
1. provisions
2. barren

Page 52
1. exuberant/excited
2. stamina/energy
3. provisions/supplies
4. summit/peak
5. hazardous/risky
6. apparel/clothing
7. barren/empty

8. encounter/meet
9. obstacle/barrier
10. essential/necessary
Answers will vary.

Page 53
1. essential
2. apparel
3. provisions
4. hazardous
5. encountered
6. obstacles
7. summit
8. barren
9. stamina
10. exuberant

Page 54
a. exuberant
b. barren,
c. summit
d. essential
e. apparel
f. hazardous
g. stamina
h. provisions
i. obstacle
j. encounter
Answer: Mount Everest

Word Whiz answers may vary. (Sample answer: height above the earth's surface)

WHAT'S SO FUNNY, TUCKER TICKLE?
Page 55
1. rambunctious
2. dillydally

Page 56
1. S 2. A 3. A 4. S 5. S
6. S 7. S 8. S 9. S 10. A
Answers will vary.

Page 57
1. bamboozled
2. hubbub
3. shenanigans
4. cantankerous
5. dillydally
6. scalawag
7. knickknacks

8. rambunctious
9. skedaddled
10. chortled

Page 58
a. knickknack
b. bamboozle
c. hubbub
d. skedaddle
e. dillydally
f. chortle
g. rambunctious
h. shenanigans
i. cantankerous
j. scalawag,
Answer: Call a tow truck.

Word Whiz answers may vary. Sample answer: very, very funny)

WE'RE ALREADY ALL READY TO GO
Page 59
1. precede
2. device

Page 60
1. S 2. S 3. A 4. S 5. S
6. A 7. A 8. A 9. S 10. A
Answers will vary.

Page 61
1. ascend
2. assent
3. devise, device
4. commended
5. commenced
6. proceed
7. precede
8. adapt
9. adept

Word Whiz: except

FROM HONKING GEESE TO HONKING HORNS
Page 63
1. populous
2. numerous

Page 64
Country – rural, pasture, graze, orchard, picturesque, (numerous, illuminated)
City – hectic, urban, populous illuminated, numerous (picturesque)
Answers will vary.

Page 65
1. rural
2. orchard
3. graze
4. pasture
5. picturesque
6. numerous
7. illuminated
8. Urban
9. hectic
10. populous

Page 66
a. pasture
b. rural
c. populous
d. illuminated
e. orchard
f. hectic
g. picturesque
h. graze,
i. urban
j. numerous
Answer: the Empire State Building

Page 62

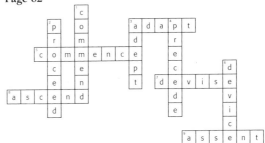

Word Whiz answers
may vary. (Sample answer:
a very tall building)

OLYMPIC GOLD
Page 67
1. structure
2. arduous

Page 68
1. structure/building
2. champion/winner
3. debut/introduction
4. extraordinary/special
5. spectator/watcher
6. symbol/representation
7. arduous /difficult
8. procession/parade
9. achievement/success
10. flawless/perfect
Answers will vary.

Page 69
1. extraordinary
2. procession
3. symbol
4. structures
5. spectators
6. arduous
7. debut
8. flawless
9. achievement
10. champion

Page 70
a. achievement
b. debut
c. flawless
d. procession
e. champion
f. symbol
g. spectator
h. arduous
i. extraordinary
j. structures
Answer: the triathlon

Word Whiz: without

THE WORD ARTIST
Page 71
1. excel
2. realistic

Page 72
1. A 2. S 3. A 4. S 5. A
6. A 7. S 8. A 9. S 10. S

Page 73
1. excelled
2. figures
3. portraits
4. ingenious
5. exhibited
6. landscapes
7. vivid
8. hues
9. realistic
10. masterpieces

Page 74
a. portrait
b. masterpiece
c. hue
d. ingenious
e. landscape
f. exhibit
g. realistic
h. excel
i. vivid
j. figure
Answer: used finger paints

Word Whiz answers may
vary. (Sample answer: a
picture of oneself made by
oneself)

IT TAKES ALL KINDS
Page 75
1. inquisitive
2. sensible

Page 76
1. A 2. S 3. A 4. S 5. S
6. S 7. A 8. A 9. A 10. A
Answers will vary.

Page 77
1. sociable
2. ambitious
3. inquisitive
4. mischievous
5. sensible
6. courteous
7. confident
8. entertaining
9. energetic
10. patient

Page 78
a. patient
b. inquisitive
c. mischievous
d. sociable
e. sensible
f. energetic
g. ambitious
h. entertaining,
i. confident,
j. courteous
k. during a brainstorm

Word Whiz answers may
vary. (Sample answer: to
try to find out by asking)

**SPEEDWELL SMART,
SUPER SLEUTH**
Page 79
1. flee
2. accomplice

Page 80
1. pursue/follow
2. culprit/wrongdoer
3. cunning/sly
4. apprehend/capture
5. disguise/costume
6. thwart/stop
7. perplexed/puzzled
8. investigation/
examination
9. flee/run off
10. accomplice/partner in
crime
Answers will vary.

Page 81
1. investigation
2. apprehend
3. culprit
4. thwarted
5. accomplice
6. disguise
7. flee
8. pursued
9. perplexed
10. cunning

Page 82
a. perplexed
b. apprehend
c. thwart
d. culprit

e. disguise
f. flee
g. investigation
h. accomplice
i. cunning
j. pursue,
Answer: fingerprints

Word Whiz answers may
vary. (Sample answer:
guilty or deserving the
blame for)

**A RAIN FOREST
EXPEDITION**
Page 83
1. detect
2. solitary

Page 84
1. foliage/leaves
2. detect/notice
3. dense/crowded
4. flourish/succeed
5. suspend/hang
6. hover/float
7. lethargic/inactive
8. vast/huge
9. audible/hearable
10. solitary/alone
Answers will vary.

Page 85
1. detect
2. suspended
3. lethargic
4. dense
5. foliage
6. flourish
7. audible
8. solitary
9. vast
10. hover

Page 86
Crossword answers will
vary.

Word Whiz answers may
vary (sample answer:
nearness closeness)

Instant Homework Packets: Vocabulary © 2010 by Jan Meyer. Scholastic Teaching Resources